WHEN
BAD
CHURCHES
HAPPEN TO
GOOD
PASTORS

WHEN
BAD
CHURCHES
HAPPEN TO
GOOD
PASTORS

WHY PASTORS LEAVE AND WHAT YOU CAN DO ABOUT IT

DAVID AND LISA FRISBIE

BEACON HILL PRESS

OF KANSAS CITY

DEDICATION

This book is dedicated to the men and women who serve us in settings of ministry: To pastors and missionaries, to superintendents and bishops, to worship leaders and youth ministers and others who grace our communities of faith.

We will mention a few of these by name, with regrets that we can't mention many more. To begin, we would like to thank some retired district superintendents we know—and we'll note that "retired" does not mean inactive! Among these we would like to honor and thank Dr. Russell and Ruth Human from the United States, Jacob and Roberta Overduin from The Netherlands, Dr. Duane and Linda Srader who served in the Azores Islands and in Portugal (as well as the United States), Dr. Danny and Bonnie Gales from Canada, Dr. Norman Bloom from the United States, Dr. Gary and Juanita Jones of New England and Florida, and Dr. Sam and Grace Pickenpaugh, who served in Australia and also in the United States.

There are others who have gone on to glory and we think of them with much respect and with great fondness. But as we write these words, the wonderful men and women who are mentioned in the paragraph above are all living, active, and serving God with much distinction. For example, Dr. Danny Gales is actively involved in a ministry that supports church leaders through prayer. He is not "retired" from serving!

We would also like to mention some retired pastors, and among these some have served in denominational offices as well. We would like to honor and thank Paul and Pauline Hicks of Canada and Minnesota, Dr. Paul and Dr. Connie Cunningham from College Church of the Nazarene in Kansas, Ken and Jennie Woods of Minnesota and Missouri, Ron and Carol McGilvra from Minnesota, Rodger and Sharon Manning of Arizona, Wes and Zelda Burns from Arkansas and Ohio, and Bill and Emily Kelvington from Florida. Among these are a general superintendent emeritus (Dr. Paul Cunningham) and the current chaplain and campus pastor of the Lakeland Holiness Camp (Rev. William Kelvington). Rodger Manning is serving a major missions organization that is based in Mesa, Arizona. Many other retired pastors we have respected have gone on to glory and we are grateful for their faithful witness. Yet as we write these words, the wonderful men and women mentioned in this paragraph are still living and still active in many types of ministry—preaching, teaching, writing, and more.

It is a bit more challenging to try to thank those who are still on active duty in their roles as pastors, missionaries, superintendents, and denominational offices. There are so many who are serving so faithfully and so well! Our efforts here will fall short. We regret that we cannot be more inclusive in these few brief paragraphs.

Among ministers who lead worship, we would like to mention Dr. Hardy Weathers, whose career also included the leadership of Nazarene Publishing House. Dr. Weathers was and is one of the most godly, Spirit-filled leaders of worship whom we have ever known! His awareness of and sensitivity to the Holy Spirit, while guiding us in corporate worship, has been a blessing to thousands of people across decades of ministry. We would like to honor and recognize Robert

Evanoff, who has guided intentional, God-focused worship for large Lutheran congregations and small Nazarene ones—and who somehow found the time to create "PortaStand"—one of the most clever and durable portable music stands we have ever seen. Bob is a composer and arranger of beautiful music, but most of all he is a worship leader with a shining, exemplary heart for God. We would like to commend Collin Campbell, who served in worship leadership even while still a student at Oral Roberts University. Since graduating, Collin has led worship for dynamic contemporary congregations including one of the larger Nazarene churches in the denomination. As with the worship leaders mentioned above, we want to note Collin's remarkable awareness of what God is doing in a service and his sensitivity to the Spirit in leading music, prayer, reflection, or a focus on the Scriptures. And after mentioning these we would like to cite the entire worship team at North Coast Church in Vista, California—literally dozens of people (perhaps hundreds—we honestly don't know the count)—who all serve in humble, God-focused worship ministry that is powerful and effective, and musically first-rate. Those who serve at North Coast take guidance and direction from Andy Na, who personifies what it means to be holy and humble, a God-seeker and a God-follower. Andy's life and music are an inspiration to everyone who knows him; he sets a good example for all of us to follow, including anyone who aspires to lead worship.

Among active pastors there are so many we would like to recognize. We will mention Jim Thornton in Oklahoma, a friend who helps us as "iron sharpens iron." Jim is an author, speaker, and deep thinker. It is always a blessing to converse with him on any topic related to church and ministry. Dr. John Whitsett has served with honor at congregations of all sizes, presenting thoughtful, well-crafted sermons that point all of us in God's direction. Brett Rickey is a creative, energizing leader who has already guided the course of two large Nazarene churches and has also authored several excellent books. Doug

Gunsalus left youth ministry in order to plant a new congregation; he is consistently among the leading-edge thinkers who help all of us understand the purpose and mission of the church. Jason Hill is a gifted church planter and a trainer of church planters; Jason writes curriculum and thinks wisely about how to help people grow in their faith. Rick Power has lived and served in China and Hawaii and now provides thoughtful, inspiring leadership to a vital church of several thousand in the center of the USA. There are so many more we would love to recognize and thank here! We could fill many more pages with our tributes. Meanwhile, all of the pastors above currently serve in "lead pastor" roles in their respective congregations.

For a brief moment, let's fly across North America and visit some caring, committed pastors who are making a difference in their local communities. Ready? Let's visit with Scott and Andrea Marshall in Missouri, Greg and Kelly Baker in North Dakota, Matt and Jeni Zimmer in Missouri, Bob and Linda Reter in Pennsylvania, Anthony and Wanda Baker in Arkansas, Paul and Heidi Haddix in Minnesota, Bill and Susan Nielson in Arizona, Dave and Lori Anderson in Illinois, Jonathan and Rondalyn Merki in New Jersey, Jason and Erica Matters in Missouri, Rodney and Tammy Amos in Texas, and Joel and Linda Atwell in Kansas. All of these couples are moving forward in ministry, leading their congregations and communities toward fullness in Christ.

Let's visit with a children's pastor who grew up in Africa and, together with his wife, is making an eternal difference in the St. Louis metro area: Randy and Lisa Calhoun. After raising their biological children, Randy and Lisa have adopted two orphans from Rwanda and are guiding a second generation toward faith. Both Randy and Lisa are active in ministry in their local church.

Among pastors who serve in staff roles, we would like to recognize and thank Chad and Stephanie Johnson in Arizona, Tomy and Mendy Cummins in Florida, and Buddy and Alicia Davis in Oklahoma. In the case of all three of these couples, both partners serve in active-duty ministry. Each brings different gifts to the mix; what these couples share in common is that both husband and wife are actively serving the congregation as associate or staff ministers.

Although we love and respect many leaders of many Celebrate Recovery ministries across North America, we would like to cite Buddy and Alicia Davis for leading the most exciting, high-energy, God-focused CR ministry we have ever experienced.

Among leaders of women's ministries we would like to honor Linda Hardin of Nashville, Tennessee, and Pam Clark of Oceanside, California. Linda and Pam lead highly effective ministry to women. Linda has served in denominational offices; Pam has led numerous missions trips to Africa and other venues.

As always, we are forever grateful to the pastoral team whose ministry shapes our lives each and every week. Our four senior pastors—Dr. Larry Osborne, Chris Brown, Dr. Charlie Bradshaw, and Paul Savona—share in oversight of a vibrant community of faith that is currently around ten thousand in number. Each of these four pastors brings a different dimension to the ministry: Larry and Chris combine for creative and inspiring teaching, Charlie provides administration and staff organization, Paul contributes leadership to ministries of caring and prayer. Between them these four senior pastors have made a permanent difference in our Christian walk.

—From the journey, *David & Lisa*

CONTENTS

ACKNOWLEDGMENTS

Sometimes we write because we're stranded somewhere, and there is little else we can do besides read, write, and pray. We mix it up; we do some of each.

We were stranded in Houston after 9/11. We had flown there for meetings of the Global Nazarene Youth International Council. We were supposed to fly on 9/11 but came down a day early, gratefully so. We had a hotel room, a rental car, and a group of good friends around us when everything changed in an instant. We ended up being in Houston longer than we planned, but we got some reading, writing, and praying done as a result.

We were stranded in London when a volcano erupted in Iceland. We had flown there en route to speak at retreats for missionaries and pastors in Bulgaria and in Kosovo. We landed safely in London, where skies were uncharacteristically beautiful, with bright sun and moderate temperatures—London at its absolute best. Despite all that, the powers that be decided that airplanes could land, but not take off again. So they grounded us for "a few hours" that ended up becoming nine very long days and nights.

Besides meeting people from all over the world, helping with language translations, Internet access, and the occasional baby-sitting while a single mom or busy dad stood in line, we ended up doing a lot of reading, writing, and praying. Being stranded gives you more time to catch up on those things. And after nine totally unexpected days and nights at Heathrow airport, we felt more than "caught up" on all of our reading, writing, and praying.

We were stranded more recently in Dallas when freak winter storms moved through the area with ferocity. We had flown there en route to Oklahoma to attend and participate in winter graduation at Southern Nazarene University. With respect to Houston and London, Dallas is a far nicer place to be stranded. The Dallas-Fort Worth (DFW) airport is beautiful and well organized; a fast and efficient SkyLink runs constantly between terminals. And, happily, you can get a burrito at DFW that rivals the world's finest. Just go to Pappasito's, near Gate 28 in the "A" terminal and sample either a Monterrey or a Tampico burrito from the "to go" menu. Either of those burritos is large enough to share with a friend, but if you're going to be stranded for a while, you may want to carb-load while you can.

Being stranded in Dallas gave us extra time to read, write, and pray, including some editing of this book you are now reading. So if there are parts of the book that make really good sense to you, thank the burritos. Or perhaps Pappasito's.

Meanwhile, we also do some writing when we're not stranded. Periodically we interrupt our schedule and set aside some blocks of time just to write and edit books, articles, and other projects. As we complete our work on this project, we want to thank four people who helped us by providing creative, writer-friendly environments for the work we needed to do.

Jerry Gering made a place available to us in the warm desert of our home state. We did some writing at Jerry's place; this book is the better because of it. Jerry's well-stocked retreat provided everything we needed to write and thrive. Jerry proved to be a gracious host; we'd stay there again anytime. Thanks, Jerry!

Rich and JoAnn Burnett made a place available to us in the avocado capital of the world—Fallbrook, California. Sharing an expansive view with three frisky golden retrievers and two new friends (Rich and JoAnn) proved to be a great aid to the process of writing and editing these pages. Thank you, Rich and JoAnn!

Noreen Van Leeuwen made a place available to us near Table Rock Lake, a sprawling and magnificent body of water in America's heartland. Outfitted with a nautical theme, Noreen's place had us waking up cheerful and smiling each day. The hard-core, down-to-the-wire editing for this book happened at Noreen's. Thank you, Noreen!

With warm thanks to Jerry, Rich, JoAnn, and Noreen, this book is now complete. We are grateful for the tranquil places and serene spaces in which we could write and edit the various stages of this project.

And also we have learned how—in whatsoever place we are stranded—to be content.

—From the journey, *David & Lisa*

ONE

FROM
GENESIS
TO
EXODUS

AFTER BRIGHT BEGINNINGS, WHY DO SO MANY PASTORS LEAVE THE MINISTRY?

Popular speaker and author John Ortberg gave the commencement address as Bethel Theological Seminary sent the Class of 2001 out into ministerial service. The seminary's beautiful chapel was packed with graduates and their families. Some of the graduating students were already serving assignments in pastoral ministry; some of these had cheering sections from among the congregations they served. The optimism and enthusiasm in Bethel's great hall was tangible and real.

Ortberg framed his remarks from the theme of one of his best-selling books. "If you want to walk on water," Ortberg told the crowd, "you've got to get out of the boat." His message was a stirring tribute to faith in action, a testament to leaving comfort behind and choosing to follow God even if facing danger and uncertainty.

Ortberg, one of the masterful speakers and authors of this generation, held the crowd's attention with stories, examples, and a well-crafted narrative. A former member of the teaching staff at Willow Creek Community Church, Ortberg was then serving as the lead pastor of his own congregation in California. His name was well known to the graduating students, and his commencement address was met with rapt attention and a flurry of note taking.

One of Bethel's stirring traditions preceded the ceremony. By long tradition and practice, Bethel's graduating students don their robes and regalia in a nearby building, a short walk away from the great hall. When they are decked out in their caps and gowns and lined up in correct alphabetical order, the graduates are then escorted outdoors through a grassy area en route to the setting of their graduation. An inspiring and special gift is waiting for them.

As they leave the robing building and emerge out into the sunlight, the graduates are met by a smiling gauntlet comprised of faculty and administration, all cheering loudly and applauding the success and future prospects of these soon-to-be graduates. The moment is unexpected and never fails to elicit a sense of shock and awe among the surprised students. Tears of joy are not uncommon among the more expressive.

It was the same on that spring day in 2001. Before seeing Ortberg, before hearing the commencement address, before the crowd could even see them arrive, graduating seminarians were spontaneously applauded and loudly cheered by their professors and faculty advisers. For many, this surprise ovation became a highlight of their entire seminary experience.

Meanwhile on that bright spring day there were other ovations to follow. There were raucous cheers for the group as a whole, as family members or friends smuggled air horns and other noisemakers into the building. There were prolonged cheers for the individual graduates as each name was read aloud by the faculty. There were photos *of* the graduates and *with* the graduates; photos of graduates standing next to proud parents or smiling spouses or restless children.

The aura of celebration and affirmation on that day was entirely appropriate and was typical of many other seminaries and Bible colleges in that same season. A fresh class of ministers was being deployed into service to local congregations, missions boards, and other settings of Christian service. The completion of all academic requirements was a cause for joy and relief among the students and for respect and congratulations among those who loved them.

Fittingly, with an author as the main speaker, a group of graduates was moving from one chapter of their lives to the next chapter, ready to experience the fulfillment and fruition of their life's calling: becoming a pastor.

With applause and affirmation echoing loudly throughout the whole campus, the brand-new graduates were sent out to serve.

Few of the graduates thought to wonder: How long will the cheering last?

Perhaps a Smattering of Applause—In the Beginning

Although traditions vary, there are some congregations that choose to welcome a new pastor with applause and affirmation. A new minister may be installed by a superintendent or bishop; there may be an all-church dinner or other event to celebrate the occasion. When a minister is being installed, there may be words of affirmation or even an invitation for the assembled group to applaud their new pastor a time or two. In larger churches there may be correspondingly larger celebrations.

One pastor, arriving to serve the largest congregation in his denomination, was driven onto the church campus in a convertible. Along a tree-lined drive the shiny new convertible made a slow and regal entry. The parade resembled halftime at a high school football game, as the campus royalty is escorted onto the field. The new pastor and his wife sat in the back of the convertible and waved to the crowd; the entire event looked much like the crowning of a homecoming king and queen.

Although some (particularly in smaller congregations) might find all of this a bit theatrical and "over the top," the celebration seemed to fit within its context. A very large group of people was welcoming a new pastor to a very prominent place of service and ministry. Since it can be difficult to individually meet and greet five or six thousand people, having an outdoor "coronation arrival" might make sense. The size and scope of the happy celebration also sends a signal to the new pastor that he or she will be appreciated, valued, and cherished. Smaller-church pastors may need to be content with a potluck dinner.

Welcoming traditions vary by theology and geography, by size and setting, and by demographics of all types. The point is, there is sometimes a smattering of applause as a new pastor arrives to serve a congregation. While usually not as raucous and celebratory as the cheering at a graduation ceremony, there can be—and arguably should be—heartfelt and spontaneous gifts of affirmation when a new minister is welcomed.

Whether by choreographed parade or lukewarm potluck, as a new minister is welcomed, there is generally a positive interval during which the arriving pastor is appreciated, or at least in which most criticism is muted or postponed. Even a highly conflicted church can call a truce or a cease-fire to welcome a new leader.

In cases where a minister is elected by a congregation, the margin of victory may signal the intensity and tone of the welcome. Where there is a clear-cut majority voting to affirm the call, there may also be a sense of affirming welcome. Where the margin of victory is inconclusive, or where a church seems divided over the choice of a new minister, the warmth of the welcome may seem more subdued.

How Long Will the Honeymoon Last?

In the literature of pastoral service the positive interlude after arrival is often described as the "honeymoon" phase of ministry. A new pastor has just arrived; he or she may be affirmed and welcomed and greeted with gifts. There may be a small or large cavalcade of positive feedback—affirming smiles, warm handshakes, and other tokens of genuine affection.

While a honeymoon phase is fairly typical of pastoral service, it is not assured or automatic. For example, when following a popular pastor who has had a long service in a particular place, the next to serve may lack a honeymoon. There may instead be a lengthy period of mourning that needs to occur before a new pastor—any new pastor—will be welcomed and appreciated.

For this reason, some in pastoral supervision (bishops, superintendents, and so on) prefer and enforce a lengthy interval following the conclusion of a longer-term pastorate. Within this interval some prefer to place established interim pastors, often retired ministers who have no personal ambition and also no interest in serving the church on a regular basis. The mere designation of someone as the interim pastor may relax the congregation and allow it to receive ministry, without making direct comparisons to what has just been "lost" in the pulpit or parish.

The situation can become particularly complex when a pastor or leader is elected to a place of regional or district denominational leadership, vacating his or her church and yet now being in presiding jurisdiction over the church and its process of pastoral replacement. It is so difficult to serve well in this situation, and stories of trials and tribulations are not uncommon in this specific situation. Some have done this well and should be congratulated and studied. Others have not fared as well in navigating these challenging waters, with resulting problems and issues in the church and with regard to the next pastor who serves it.

Despite these and other exceptions, the general trend in pastoral ministry is for the new leader to enjoy some sort of honeymoon period as he or she arrives to serve in a new setting. During the arrival process, the congregation may tend to notice the strengths and gifts of a minister instead of focusing on what he or she seems to lack in skill sets or aptitude. The resulting season is not unlike the early days of a good marriage, before reality sets in.

It is entirely possible to move from being a celebrated seminary graduate, applauded and affirmed, to being a new pastor in a new place, welcomed and appreciated and valued. Such a process and outcome is not uncommon, yet it would be a huge mistake to interpret applause and affirmation as illustrating the normative pathways that one travels in ministry. Rare is the pastor who generates ongoing applause and affirmation over a long-term service to a congregation. Instead the more usual pattern is for a new minister to be warmly welcomed, genuinely appreciated, and then over time to be somewhat taken for granted, or perhaps even opposed outright as he or she attempts to lead and guide the church.

It may be quantifiably accurate to suggest that for most pastors in most places, the honeymoon phase will be a season of ministry but not an enduring and ongoing reality. When the honeymoon is over—whether it lasts three months, six months, twelve months, or eighteen months into the new relationship—it may be replaced by apathy, malaise, criticism, or political maneuvering among the congregants.

Much like someone who is sipping an energy drink and enjoying the buzz, pastors may discover that after the initial surge or rush is over there is a falling off, a winding down, or a lapse of the overall energy level. Depending on the situation and setting, there may even be a crash or a sense of depression that sets in as the caffeinated energy burns away and reality emerges into full view.

Speed Dating

Although it's a topic for quite another book overall, pastoral ministry is a great environment for growing up, for maturing as a person, and for conforming more fully to the image of Christ. Yet we should also note that some persons arrive in pastoral ministry having only recently begun—or perhaps having not quite started yet—the difficult path to maturity. The less mature the pastor, the less perceptive he or she may be in realizing that the end of the honeymoon phase is a normal adaptive process that both the pastor and the congregation must work through.

Accordingly, a less mature pastor may find himself or herself in a fight or flight mind-set, engaging too quickly in conflict and disagreement or fleeing too swiftly to another church or setting. We'll discuss the fight options in much more detail within the second section of this book. For this chapter, we'll look at the tendency to take flight and move to another setting or leave ministry entirely.

One pastor in the Midwest had served three settings in less than five years when he announced his resignation from the third setting. He was able to find yet another opportunity, then yet another, and at the ten-year mark of his ministry he was ready to resign from his fifth church. This particular pastor seemed intelligent, sincere in his faith, and in many ways gifted for ministry. Yet time after time and place after place, this pastor showed up for the "Sunday night surprise," announcing a resignation that caught the congregation off guard.

This pattern may be possible to sustain for a brief time, especially if the minister is young or seems highly gifted. However, it is not possible to sustain this pattern over the longer term. Sooner or later bishops, superintendents, or other denominational leaders are not willing to install such a temporary minister, forcing yet another congregation to grieve a premature loss. Taking flight very swiftly from one church to another may work for a season; it will probably not hold up for a lifetime of service.

In quite a few other cases there is a similar dynamic in play, yet with longer terms of service between the changes in assignment. This occurs because some pastors are savvy enough to realize that a series of short durations in ministry may look bad to those in denominational supervision. There is a widely held belief among pastors that departing a place after two years is too soon while leaving after three or four years is acceptable. Therefore the more astute disappointed or disillusioned pastors may simply wait out the duration before taking flight to a new location or setting. During the gap between "too soon" and "acceptable," many of these ministers may merely be marking time. While continuing to serve, they are busy sending out résumés in hopes of gauging interest in their services.

Ministry professionals talk about the "aquarium shifting," which occurs when believers move from one church to another, simply transferring Christians (fish) from one church (tank) to the next. Yet there is a similar phenomenon by which ministers shift tanks too— running from one disappointment to a brand-new setting, only to be freshly disappointed. Ask any working superintendent about this, and he or she can describe many such cases, usually from recent or current memory.

Such pastors are doing something like speed dating, rushing from one relationship to the next relationship, not stopping long enough to ever become fully or meaningfully connected. Or as one retired denominational leader described it, such pastors are like "serial adulterers" (his words) because they won't stay faithful to any given assignment but are quickly bored, disinterested, and looking around.

"I wouldn't hire those kinds of pastors," the same retired leader tells us as we interview him for this book. "I inherited a few who wanted to always keep shifting around within the districts I served, and sometimes that did happen," he admits. "But I wouldn't bring in that kind of mind-set from the outside and add it to my existing pastoral team. I was more protective than that! I wanted my pastors to learn from each other in a positive way. I wanted them to see and emulate positive patterns in ministry—not serial adultery!"

Whether from immaturity, disillusionment, or unrealistic expectations, some ministers change places often and repeatedly. They thrive on the buzz of a new relationship, and then when the inevitable crash occurs, they move on. So perhaps instead of speed daters or "serial adulterers," these ministers could be thought of as "adulation addicts" or "honeymoon hoppers." Regardless of the tag or label we apply, this kind of behavior in ministry can be a career killer.

Just One Door—No Revolving

Still other pastors leave ministry altogether when the going gets tough, finding other ways to feed their family. In these first few decades of the twenty-first century, there is much more "exodus" than there is "genesis" in pastoral ministry—that is, more men and women are departing from ministry than are enrolling in ministry. This results in the closing of churches, the consolidation of parishes, and in some cases a return to the long ago "circuit-rider" model by which one pastor serves more than one congregation.

Up close, the patterns and trends are not encouraging. Data from the Fuller Institute, the Barna Group, and other observers affirms the following census of pastoral realities:

- More than four thousand new churches are planted each year, yet more than seven thousand existing churches are closed annually.[1]
- More than seventeen hundred pastors exit the ministry each month.[2]
- Many denominations report an empty pulpit crisis—that is, there are not enough trained pastors to serve the churches that already exist.

While the above data is focused on Protestant expressions of the Christian faith, the Roman Catholic Church finds itself in a similar situation. There are not enough priests to supply the parishes, with the result that the laity or other religious workers such as nuns are pressed into essential clerical duties.

"The harvest is plentiful but the workers are few," Matthew reports in his Gospel account (9:37). While written two millennia ago, Matthew's analysis accurately describes our contemporary church life. There are not enough laborers (pastors) to serve the churches that already exist. Pulpits stand empty and parishes close or consolidate. Viewed through the lens of doing pastoral ministry, one aspect of the problem is that so many laborers are leaving the harvest fields. Without passing judgment on these once-called servants we can merely note that the supply of laborers seems to be decreasing, not increasing, which means the problem will only get worse.

While it may be impossible to address all of the related issues within the context of one volume, this book arrives to discuss the cluster of problems that occur when a pastor encounters a difficult place to serve. Even while doing the research and writing for this project, we've received many suggestions that we should write a sequel called *When Bad Pastors Happen to Good Churches*.

To be sure, there are difficult pastors also. There are immature ministers and youthful seminarians with unrealistic expectations about life in the ministry. There are stubborn and hardheaded pastors, for whom "my way or the highway" seems to be an operating mantra. There are dictatorial pastors and lazy pastors and a wide range of other types of misfits in ministry. Since the pool of pastoral ministry is drawn from the wider pool called human beings, such results are inevitable.

In the experience of these authors, the overwhelming majority of pastors that we encounter are well-motivated, well-intentioned, and often also well-trained. They are reasonably mature (adjusting for age and experience) and usually flexible in their approaches to problems and solutions. And although our work as counselors often connects us with pastors in crisis, situations in which we may see pastors at their worst, the broader reality is that we have immense respect for those who serve in ministry. Over time, and despite our experience with casualties and cases, our respect for pastors has only grown deeper and fuller.

We love, respect, and value those who serve us in pastoral ministry. They are competent, caring men and women with huge hearts for God, genuine compassion for others, and a desire to see the body of Christ built up and encouraged.

These great men and women enter into pastoral practice with high hopes and a true desire to make a difference in this world. Yet all too often these same men and women find themselves depleted, exhausted, and searching for an exit strategy. The culling process by which pastors depart from pastoral ministry is in no sense Darwinian in nature—it does not seem to be the "fittest" who may survive, and it does not appear to be the "misfits" who may depart. Instead, a look at those who leave pastoral ministry reveals many types and temperaments, many levels of intelligence and education, many backgrounds and prior experiences. What these departing servants seem to have in common is their departure—and little else.

So although this book begins with Genesis—a joyous and celebratory graduation day at a seminary—the bulk of the book deals with Exodus instead. Our primary focus in these pages will be this one: Why are so many pastors leaving the ministry in this current hour and what can we do about it?

Questions for Reflection

In each chapter, we will include questions geared toward three different leadership groups within the church: pastors and ministers, local churches and church boards, and denominational leaders (superintendents, bishops, and so on). These questions will help you apply the lessons learned in each chapter to your own life.

Pastors and Ministers

1. In the course of a typical month, how often do you mentally consider leaving your current assignment and seeking a new congregation to serve and lead? How much time do you invest in thinking about these types of possibilities?

2. In the course of a typical month, how often do you mentally consider leaving the ministry and becoming employed elsewhere in a religious or secular setting but not in direct ministry to a local congregation? When you have these thoughts (if you do) how long do you typically indulge the underlying feelings? How long do these thoughts tend to last?

3. How many of your friends or former classmates have started out in pastoral ministry but have since left that venue of service and chosen another profession, vocation, or calling? In your view, did God himself call these pastors to depart from pastoral ministry, or did these persons merely get tired, discouraged, worn out, or exhausted from constant conflict and ongoing issues within their local settings?

4. If you chose to depart from pastoral ministry, do you believe that your spouse and family would be supportive of this change? If you left pastoral ministry as a vocation, do you believe that your parents, mentors, former college or seminary professors, and others would understand?

5. If you have ever departed from one congregation in order to go and serve another, were you restless, searching, or ready to leave before the departure actually happened? If so, about how long were you restless before the "deliverance" occurred?

6. If you have ever departed from one congregation in order to go and serve another, did upward mobility—that is, moving to a larger church, a better rate of pay, or a more prominent place—factor into your decision?

7. In order to leave pastoral ministry as a vocation, would you personally need as strong a sense of calling from God in order to depart, as you did in order to accept God's original call? Why or why not?

8. Informally, some churches have come to be called "clergy killers" because of the number of ministerial casualties reported there. If you were in supervision or jurisdiction over a church with a "clergy killer" reputation, how might you approach the congregation or its leaders? Would you knowingly and willingly serve such a church as their pastor?

Local Churches and Church Boards

1. When a pastor decides to leave your congregation, are you usually surprised by his or her decision, or have you usually seen it coming with regard to the prospective departure of a pastor who is serving you?

2. Although a congregation gets to vote when a pastor is called, in most cases a congregation does not get to vote on whether a pastor can leave to accept a new assignment within the denomination. To what extent—if any—do you wish that a congregation could vote to allow a minister to leave or vote to prevent this departure?

3. When there is conflict in the congregation, or when a pastor gets crosswise with key leaders within the church, there is often a pastoral departure without going through any kind of formal process or mediation. In traditions where pastors are reviewed every few years, a pastor may choose to depart after having a bad review. Still other pastors choose to depart before being formally and officially reviewed so that a bad review does not become a stain on their permanent records. Do you wish that there were some kind of intervention by the district or the denomination when a pastor's ministry seems to be derailing or losing traction, with the goal of helping the church hold and keep its pastor for effective service? Or are you more comfortable simply letting pastors go and hoping for the best in your next minister?

4. How often does the presence of a new (incoming) pastor resolve the core or underlying issues or tensions within a congregation? When you change the face in the pulpit and the pastor's name on the church sign, does the church itself change, or is the congregation still much the same in terms of its overall dynamics, health (or lack of health), and issues?

5. In your view, do pastors leave too often, or not often enough? In your view, is it even possible for a church to keep a pastor for the duration of his or her ministry, or are you already resigned to the fact that your better and more effective pastors will probably keep climbing the ladder to bigger and better places of service?

Denominational Leaders

1. Across the arc of your leadership and service, would you say that the pool of available pastors who might serve a local congregation has increased or decreased, in terms of quantity? Is it easier or harder to fill a church now?

2. Would you rather populate your own district with new (inexperienced) pastors or with pastors who have served for a decade or more? In your view, which category of pastor (inexperienced versus experienced) is a better fit for most of the churches under your direct care?

3. To what extent do you believe the global church (denomination, movement, or organization) would be wise to retain and revitalize those who are already serving in ministry, versus allowing the exodus to continue? Are you aware of any positive or successful efforts (structured, ongoing) to retain pastors for ministerial service?

4. How thorough are the exit interviews that you conduct when someone leaves a place of ministry on your own district? To what extent do you attempt to personally drill down to explore the underlying causes behind or beneath the departure of a local pastor? Do you believe that you are usually successful in understanding the true dynamics that are in play when a pastor leaves?

5. When an experienced pastor wants to transfer into your district and wishes to be available to serve a church under your care, what are the key issues that you try to understand regarding that pastor's previous service to other congregations in other places? To what extent do you explore or consider congregational conflict or unresolved issues of pastoral health (emotional or spiritual) as you consider welcoming a transferring minister to your district?

TWO

MISSING
THE
PROMISED
LAND

THE CONSEQUENCES AND OUTCOMES OF
SHORT-TERM PASTORATES AND MINISTRIES

What happens to a church when their pastor stays for only a short time? What happens to a congregation when a series of pastors all stay for only a short time and then leave to take other (perhaps more lucrative) assignments? What are the outcomes when a linear sequence of short-term ministers is written across the margins of the church's life experience and history? These questions are worthy of a doctoral thesis—or several.

Meanwhile, within these pages let's open the windows of history and look inside at a small church in a rural area. As with many churches in many places, there are key lay leaders and volunteers who have served the church for all of these decades and whose faithfulness is responsible for the church's ongoing existence.

Our actual case study church, as we peer through its arched Gothic windows searching for insight and wisdom, has been served by eleven pastors during the thirty-year span of time that we are considering. If we prefer, we can slice off a different thirty-year stretch and elevate the count to thirteen pastors across those specific three decades. Either way, the trend is clearly visible to even a casual, untrained observer.

Doing the math very quickly, one can determine that the average length of pastoral tenure at this church is less than three years. Although these pastors have tended to be younger (in general) and came to this church at earlier stages in their ministerial careers (with a few exceptions), the eleven ministers in question share few commonalities in terms of personality, temperament, preaching style, or other markers. Given a cohort of eleven ministers—all of them male—one finds quite a remarkable variety of styles and types and ages and personalities.

One particularly charismatic pastor, seemingly destined for a successful career in sales or multi-level marketing, passed through the church in exactly seventeen months. He accepted a larger and more prestigious assignment, then another, and then another. He continues to serve in ministry and across the breadth of his career one can see advance and ascent, when measuring in statistics such as attendance, total funds raised, new members welcomed, and other common metrics of "success" in pastoral ministry.

One older minister, who served the church in his last few days until his retirement, is the record holder by leading this church for nearly four and a half years. If we remove this minister from the cohort, we are left with ten pastors in roughly twenty-five years of this congregation's history. The minister who retired remained in this community and continued to attend this church, seemingly a positive presence and a supportive person with regard to his successors in ministry.

One aggressive and well-organized pastor formulated a twenty-year plan for ministry shortly after arriving to serve this congregation. He made large graphics of the plan, with four giant panels each representing a five-year stretch of the overall twenty-year presentation. He placed these graphics in a very prominent place inside the sanctuary so that as worshipers came and went, each could see a visual and very detailed analysis of the future twenty-year trajectory of the church.

The worshipers came and went, and noticed.

The pastor came—and then went—in a little less than two years.

During the interim after that particular pastor left, the board members voted to take the twenty-year plan down from its vaunted position on the sanctuary walls. The panels were placed in storage for a brief while, then later discarded permanently. The next few pastors who served this church did not consult, refer to, or make any inquiries about the former twenty-year outline of future success in ministry.

Although an exact study of mission statements has not been done within this community of faith, the authors are aware of at least six separate mission statements that were formulated, endorsed, and then distributed throughout the congregation during the three decades that are under consideration here. Each mission statement was separate from the others; several of them were in direct conflict with each other. From the standpoint of a lay member of the congregation, this recurring change in focus may have been confusing, or it may have been merely ignored.

There were modest fluctuations in attendance over the thirty years being studied here, but when one looks at the graph for the full three decades, the trend line shows a gradual but steady and consistent descent in key markers such as attendance, giving, evangelism, and others. So in the case of this specific church and its life history, an era in which eleven pastors labored for thirty years resulted in a steady and measurable decline in the size and financial capacity of this group.

How Long Does It Take a Pastor to Become Effective?

Dr. H. B. London, long known as a "pastor to pastors" while he served in key leadership roles at Focus on the Family, believes that a pastor's most effective ministry occurs during years five through fourteen of that pastor's service to the congregation. This does not mean that there is no fruitfulness or productivity in the earlier years, but merely that the most meaningful and measurable impact happens after relationships have been built, trust has been established between a pastor and the community of faith, and key leaders have aligned themselves with the priorities and practices of the pastor who is serving the congregation.[1]

In reality, it takes a while to build trust between a pastor and a congregation. Estimates for the general duration of this trust-building process—when it proves to be successful—vary between the five years that Dr. London proposes and a range of six or seven years suggested by others.

Scholar Joseph Umidi is among those who propose a six-year time frame. In Umidi's opinion, "Research shows that the most effective and enriching church ministries are those led by pastors who have invested at least six years in the same church community."[3]

Viewed together, London's "five to fourteen years" and Umidi's "at least six years in the same church community" point us in the direction of a sturdy and visible precept. The typical pastor arriving to serve a new community should not expect to immediately receive the trust and faithfulness of the congregation. Instead, after the pastor has served for an extended period of time, his or her integrity and walk of faith begin to be respected and well regarded by those who are being served. The result is a deposit of trust that is made in the pastor's ministry so that he or she becomes more effective in leadership and more fruitful in ministerial functions.

Other scholars affirm and supplement these observations. Glenn Ludwig, writing in his book *In It for the Long Haul: Building Effective Long-Term Pastorates,* affirms the trend of these other observations. He proposes a slightly longer duration—seven years—as the point where measurable changes in effective ministry can be quantified and observed.

Ludwig asserts that "after seven years of faithful, dedicated and consistent ministry, noticeable things begin to happen. By now, the pitch and tone of the congregation has been influenced by the pastor's style. The leadership of the church should begin to reflect the priorities and passions of a working relationship with the pastor. The dues have been paid."[4]

London, Wiseman, Umidi, and Ludwig all affirm the same principles with regard to the relationship that exists between the pastor and the congregation and also between the pastor and key leaders. The building of trust, the revelation of character, and the unity and alignment of priority and values does not occur overnight. Rather, there is steady progress in this direction over a period of time. While there may not be a magic number or a precise formula, these and other scholars suggest that a gestation period of approximately five to seven years should be considered normative and usual.

How Long Are Pastors Serving the Same Church?

A variety of contemporary studies affirm that the average tenure for today's pastors is less than four years. Some studies peg the typical length of stay at just under three years; others move the total just above three years. Most studies seem to fall within the same general range.

One of the more reliable reporters of pastoral trends, Thom Rainer, quoted a study from LifeWay Research in his recent blog post. Rainer quoted the LifeWay study as finding that the current average tenure for pastors (2012-13) stands at 3.6 years.[2] This finding is well within the norms and metrics reported by others.

In the anecdotal case study we cited earlier in this chapter, a total of eleven pastors served a rural church in a span of just three decades. Using a different three decades for the same church, there were thirteen separate pastors. It's easy to do the math for this specific place and discover that for this congregation, the average tenure of their pastors was less than three years.

Whether we look through the lens of how long a congregation is served, or whether we consider the problem from the perspective of how long a pastor stays in one place, the results are the same. There is a stunning amount of turnover in today's pulpits. If the LifeWay research is correct—and it seems very much in line with other studies—then when a new pastor arrives to serve in any given congregation, one could set the countdown clock to four years. According to these statistics, before the four years has passed the pastor will be gone.

For the remainder of this book, when we consider the question of average pastoral tenure, we will use the LifeWay Research study, resulting in a figure of 3.6 years as the duration. And since some pastors do stay in one place for a long period of time, it's obvious that other pastors must depart from places in less than 3.6 years in order to make this the average tenure.

What Happens When Pastoral Stays Are Short?

Or perhaps a better question might be: What doesn't happen?

What level of fruitful ministry never has time to emerge and develop? What amount of trust between pastor and leaders and between pastor and congregation never has time to be built? What unity of leadership, what alignment around shared priorities never develops because not enough time has passed?

We will look at the impact of short pastoral stays in terms of several different cohorts and contexts, beginning with the people who are growing up in the parsonage of the local church.

1. The effect of short pastoral stays on pastoral families

In our work as coordinators of Marriage and Family Ministries for the global Church of the Nazarene, we have served as facilitators, counselors, and plenary session speakers for retreats and camps serving the adolescent children of pastors and missionaries. We have met with, listened to, and spoken to assemblies of students around the globe. Not only is this among our favorite settings of ministry and among our favorite ways to serve the church, but it is also an amazing way to learn about pastoral families and how to help them.

In a smaller-group setting, we often do an exercise that is non-directed and also hopefully non-threatening. In many different settings and places we have passed out blank sheets of paper with some markers or crayons. Without suggesting any specific image or pointing to any definite artistic expression, we give the students this assignment: Draw us your life in pictures, starting from birth until now.

Some of the students immediately smile and begin creating art. Others sit staring blankly into space, waiting for inspiration. After a while, there is a whole room full of markers or crayons, passing over the surfaces of many pages, creating life stories in art.

After a given period of time, we assemble the small group together so that the students can, if they so choose, show us their art and tell us the story that the images reveal. This participation is voluntary and unforced.

In one of our more memorable uses of this exercise, a bright eighth grade girl drew four big yellow trucks. Nothing else was on her sheet of paper—just four very large yellow trucks. When it was her turn to speak to the group, she held up her sheet of paper. All of us gazed at a realistic rendering of four large yellow trucks. She pointed to the first truck, located at the top of the page. "This is when we moved from [name of church and city]," she told us. Pointing to the next truck she did the same. "This is when we moved from [name of church and city]." Twice more she repeated the same process, until she had told us about four churches her father had served and four times the family had moved. This somewhat introverted and shy eighth grader told us that her father was now serving his fifth church. Without prompting from anyone, she quietly told us, "I'm just waiting for the fifth truck to pull up in our driveway. It will probably happen any time now."

A sudden quietness fell on the group as a whole, then a couple of other girls walked over to give her a hug. As the eighth grader began to cry, this specific group entered into a lively discussion on how hard it is to move from one place to another—and how often they all had experienced this very same trauma.

"I am afraid to make new friends," said one teenage pastor's child. "What's the point? I just get attached to someone, we get close, and then my family moves to a new place."

"I think we're just about to move, right now," said a short seventh grade boy. "We've been talking about it as a family, and I think all of us are just about ready for our next move."

One by one these spiritually sensitive, God-centered youth shared their experiences of moving frequently, forming short-term friendships, and perpetually being the new kid both in both school and church.

When we consider pastoral tenure and pastoral service as the larger body of Christ, is this what we're hoping for? Are we hoping that the children and teens who live in our parsonages will constantly have to move around, change churches and schools, tear themselves away from old friends and try to make new ones? Is this our highest aspiration for those who serve us in ministry and for their families?

2. The effect of short pastoral stays on congregations

If London, Ludwig, and others are correct in revealing that a pastor's most effective ministry emerges after five to seven years in the same place, then congregations whose pastors depart after two or three years are not likely to experience the most effective, most fruitful aspects and outcomes of ministry.

After having a series of pastors with short stays, a congregation may decline in its willingness to trust, follow, or even respect an incoming pastor. The trend may be to regard the next pastor as a temp worker who is only going to be around for a short while. Accordingly, the congregation may tacitly or explicitly hold back from fully embracing and fully trusting its minister.

Ludwig affirms this reality. He writes that "trust is rarely established in any meaningful depth when folks believe their pastor will be 'here today and gone tomorrow.'"[5] Instead, Ludwig speaks of the value that accrues when a congregation believes and expects that its pastor will be with them for the long haul.

One of the most effective pastors we've known served a very small rural community in the northern Midwest. Across the span of his life and the church's existence, the congregation never grew to a size that would put it on the radar of *Outreach* magazine, the Barna Report, or other studies of large and thriving churches. However, when compared to the size of the town in which it was located, the church grew to large proportions indeed. Within that community, everyone knew this particular pastor. He was widely and highly respected within the church and within his community.

His service to the community—including the police department, the school board, the fire department, and many other venues—made him a visible and much-loved public figure. When he died, his funeral was one of the largest events the town and the church had ever experienced.

This pastor lived and demonstrated what Eugene Peterson has called "a long obedience in the same direction." To add to Peterson's concept, this pastor also experienced "a long obedience in the same setting." The result of this pastor's life was a harvest that will not be measured until eternity and, from the congregation's perspective, many seasons of fruitful and effective witness and ministry.

If we think about life and ministry from the congregation's point of view, the local church is best served when the door to the parsonage is not, in any sense, a revolving door.

3. The effect of short pastoral stays on ministers

In interviews with dozens of former pastors, we often heard ministers tell us that their dreams for ministry had not been realized or that their time in ministry did not turn out to be what they were hoping for. The trend was quite significant, crossing boundaries of geography and demographics. Those who had left pastoral ministry—and particularly those who left the ministry after experiencing conflict in the congregation—often told us of their sadness or sorrow with regard to ministry outcomes.

If we do not think about the children growing up in their homes, if we do not consider the needs or best interests of the congregation, if we narrow our focus only to the men and women who serve in settings of pastoral ministry, are short pastoral stays a desirable outcome for those who serve? And what does it mean when a pastor leaves a congregation after serving for only a brief length of time?

A personally charming and highly gifted pastor arrived to serve at his second church. His tenure at his first church? A mere six months. While some might have seen this as a danger signal or a warning sign, the pastor in question had a ready excuse for his short duration of service at the first setting.

Based in no small part on his attractive appearance, his personal charm, and his evident gifts for ministry, he was warmly embraced by his second church despite his scant quantity of prior service.

He was also warmly embraced by one of the women in his new community—someone who, like him, was gifted and attractive. Within only a few months in this new setting—his second church—he was involved in an extramarital affair with this woman. Meanwhile, he was leading and guiding his new church in ways that looked and seemed effective—at least on the surface. The church was growing and the outward markers of success were in place.

The pastor would serve for more than a year before his affair was discovered. Only then, after his marriage ended and a messy divorce shattered yet another pastoral home, did it become known that he had left the first setting of ministry to get away from an entanglement there.

Happily, not all short-term stays in ministry are rooted in the need to flee from an affair. Yet in a way, these short-term stays do highlight potential relationship issues. Is the pastor afraid of making a commitment to a given body of believers? Is he or she wary of being transparent and becoming known, preferring instead to hide behind qualities such as giftedness in the pulpit, personal attractiveness, or abilities in leading worship?

If the ministry is a great setting in which to grow up and become more mature, then pastors benefit when they remain in place, become known as they are, and learn to trust others while earning the trust of those they serve. This process is not for the weak or the faint of heart: It takes courage and commitment, plus a willingness to admit frailties.

Pastors who practice and model transparency and vulnerability, willing to become known as they are—warts and all—are building the foundation for powerful and effective ministry. Pastors who form deep and meaningful relationships based on mutual trust, shared accountability, demonstrated character, and integrity are setting the stage for the most rewarding and fulfilling ministry that they may have ever experienced in their lives.

It is certainly in the best interest of ministers to know and to be known, to participate in community life in ways that are authentic, and to model the spiritual disciplines and daily graces of the Christian walk in ways that are transparent and real. With the exception of a very few megachurch pastors, who function more like corporate CEOs than like shepherds of a well-known flock, ministers are much more effective when they are loved and trusted because they are known and respected.

If London, Ludwig, and others are correct in their analysis, it takes five or six or seven years of faithful service before this level of trust and impact begins to emerge and expand. This does not downplay the meaning and value of the previous years; these are setting the stage. What matters is to remain in place over the longer term, being faithful and reliable and committed. Over time, fruitfulness happens.

———

Here in Southern California where we live, we are surrounded by many groves of avocado trees. We love the fruit of these trees, and we are ardent admirers of the avocado and its many uses as a food, including zesty guacamole!

If you plant an avocado tree from seed, it will take anywhere from five to thirteen years before the tree is mature enough to bear fruit. After five years or so the tree will begin to drop blooms, but these blooms may fall off without ever becoming fruit. Eventually the fruit emerges and the tree is fully productive—seven or ten or twelve years after the seed was planted in your backyard or in the grove.

Perhaps churches are like avocado trees. As we arrive and begin to plant trees, we can expect a duration of five to thirteen years (or fourteen per H. B. London) before ripe, beautiful fruit is being produced.

Every stage leading up to that fruitful season is important and necessary, but what a great folly it is if we chop down the tree too soon or abandon the grove to ruin without staying in place long enough to reap the harvest.

Questions for Reflection

Pastors and Ministers

1. Recall the story of the eighth grade girl who drew a picture of four big yellow moving trucks and told us, "I'm just waiting for the fifth truck to arrive." Did any part of her experience or life story resonate with you? Would it resonate in the hearts and minds of the kids you are raising in your home? Why or why not?

2. Have you ever stayed at a church just to avoid having to move your kids from one place to another or from one school to another? In other words, has the potential negative impact on your family ever kept you from escaping an unpleasant or unfruitful place of service by your own deliberate choice? How much do you weigh the impact on your family when considering a possible move?

3. In your true heart, would you love to watch your kids grow up in the same school district, from K through 12? Why or why not? To what extent are you personally wired to prefer longevity in one place? Or are you one of those pastors for whom the word "restless" is an apt descriptor?

4. If you truly believed Dr. H. B. London's assertion that maximum power and effectiveness in ministry occurs during years five through fourteen in the same location, would this belief make you more likely to stay, endure hardship, work through conflicts, and then be there for the "payoff" during those later years? Why or why not?

5. If it were completely up to you (setting aside all other factors), would you prefer to remain in your current assignment or to move to some new place of service? Regardless of your answer, does anyone else know how you feel about this? Could anyone else (spouse,

family, or friend) accurately predict your answer because of knowing you so well?

6. If you have friends who have moved around a lot during their various pastoral ministries, do you regard their service as highly effective in an overall sense, or do you believe they have failed to achieve their maximum potential due to the frequent changes in venue?

7. When you hear of a pastor staying twenty or thirty years in one location, do you wish it were you? Why or why not?

8. In your view, why does it take so long for effectiveness in ministry to emerge? Do you believe that there are "shortcuts" to effective ministry or that someone could gain a high level of effectiveness in only a few months or perhaps in a year or two? Why or why not?

Local Churches and Church Boards

1. One board member of a small church told us that each new pastor changed the direction of the church and that this happened "so often, I got whiplash!" This was a very telling remark about how each incoming pastor made major changes in mission statement, worship style, times of service, and other aspects of church life, which the church then had to adjust to. Have you found it so? Has your own church experienced frequent changes in ministry and focus due to pastoral turnover? Have you experienced this type of "whiplash" due to the suddenness or frequency of this change?

2. If there were a book in print called *How to Keep Your Pastor Forever*, would you be likely to read the book? Are you interested in learning how to keep your pastor in place, serving your congregation over the long term?

3. Why would a pastor want to stay in your community, or continue serving your congregation? Have you ever adopted a specific strategy or tried a particular approach to keeping your pastor over the long term? What is or might be attractive about your setting or church, from the pastor's perspective or from the perspective of the pastor's family?

4. Simply stated, do you consider your church to be "pastor friendly"? Why or why not? What does this phrase mean to you?

Denominational Leaders

1. Do you agree with Glen Ludwig, Joseph Umidi, and others who assert that a pastor's primary effectiveness begins to emerge after five or six years of service in the same setting or location? Do you find it so? Have you observed the trend reported by Dr. H. B. London that a pastor's greatest seasons of fruitfulness in ministry tend to occur in years five through fourteen of serving in the same location?

2. Have you charted the average tenure of pastors on your district over the past one or two decades? Do you know the average length of service in their current assignments for the pastors who are serving under your jurisdiction right now? How long have your pastors been in their current places, on average? Is the average length of service moving upward or downward in your area of responsibility?

3. Do you have a strategy in place for helping your region achieve higher and higher averages in pastoral tenure? Do you have programs in position that help pastors remain encouraged for ministry, committed to their assignments, and energized for the daily race? How do you equip your pastors to endure and thrive over the long run of pastoral ministry?

4. Is it a red flag for you when a pastor who wishes to serve in your region has a history of short tenures in each previous assignment where he or she has served? Why or why not?

5. Do you maintain a ministry to the families in your parsonages, particularly for the children or teens who are growing up in the homes of your pastors? Do you have retreats, camps, events, or other programs in place for pastors' or missionaries' children and teenagers? Do you know of such programs elsewhere?

6. Do you monitor the health of pastoral spouses? Do you meaningfully serve and equip the pastoral marriages in your region, helping each marriage move toward better and abiding health? How do you do so? What programs and resources do you have in place to support pastoral marriages and to provide encouragement to pastoral spouses?

THREE
LAMENTATIONS
PAIN, REGRET, AND DAMAGE CONTROL AFTER A MINISTRY ENDS

Snow glistens on the high peaks of the mountain range as our United Airlines flight circles high above the airport, waiting for our arrival gate to open up. We enjoy the chance to admire these views; our flight is running early anyway. Even with this brief delay we will be landing ahead of schedule.

A scant forty-five minutes later we're having coffee with a former minister. We're in a bustling Starbucks location; the line is six or eight people deep. We have waited a few minutes before finding an empty table. Yet in the midst of so much activity and surrounded by so many people, there is a sense of privacy and a sense that sharing openly is safe here. Even so, before he begins telling us about his struggles, we remind our good friend that by his own choice he will remain anonymous in these pages.

"I can finally talk about these things," he tells us after we have exchanged greetings and started the interview, "without having all of my usual symptoms."

We ask him what he means by "symptoms."

"For at least a couple of years after I was run out of [name of church]," he explains, "I kept having some strange symptoms. Pretty much every time I started to talk about the problems there or what the issues had been with my leaving, all of a sudden my chest would tighten and my heart would start pounding. Sometimes I would begin to physically tremble. I wouldn't be able to stop.

"I would be standing there trying to talk to somebody—a friend or my wife's parents or someone else that I trusted—and suddenly my whole body would start to shake. I could not control the random trembling or my pulse rate or the feeling of tightness in my chest. It was like my body was reacting entirely on its own, without being under my control at all."

He stops for a moment and looks at us to gauge our response. Unknown to our friend, we've heard about symptoms like this before.

"Mike (not his real name)," we respond. "Would you believe you are at least the fifth or sixth former pastor who has told us about having these very same physical symptoms when they were trying to talk about what happened to them in their churches? In fact, the descriptions we've heard before sound almost identical to what you are telling us today."

Mike is visibly surprised; he relaxes and slumps back in his chair.

"Wow," he says softly. "I had no idea that other ex-pastors might have these same kinds of reactions while talking about what happened to them. All this time I've thought I must be a little bit weird."

He pauses for a moment of reflection.

"It kind of tells you a lot, doesn't it?" he reflects. "It kind of shows you how deeply felt these things are. I am not a melodramatic person, but there was one time, maybe six months after everything was over, that I actually thought I was having a heart attack. I was talking to my wife's dad—he was and is a huge supporter of me and my ministry—and I thought I was going to die right there on the spot. My heart was racing and then it skipped some beats. I felt flushed and warm and my heart was just racing."

In the next few moments as Mike describes his symptoms, we are grateful to learn that he did not, in fact, have a heart attack. He did, however, develop cardiac arrhythmia in the aftermath of extensive church conflict and an eventual forced exit from ministry with a specific congregation. His condition developed even though he had left the ministry and was no longer serving as a pastor anywhere, let alone in the "problem church."

Without being overly technical, you can file this under posttraumatic stress disorder and you won't be missing the mark by much. We are dealing here with symptoms that emerge not in the heat of the battle or the crisis of the moment but much later, after the fact, when the battle is over and the crisis has passed.

Later in the interview Mike tells us how grateful he is to learn that other former pastors have symptoms like his: an accelerated pulse, a marked shortness of breath, or even physically trembling and shaking while trying to tell their personal stories of conflict and loss. We assure him all over again that his physiological reactions are not unique to him or to his situation. They are symptomatic of other ministers in other places, as these gifted and God-called pastors react to memories that are laced with strong emotions. The deeper the emotional strength of the memories, the more likely it is that the physical symptoms will emerge.

When the emotions are laced with powerful emotional overtones such as fear, anger, guilt or resentment, the physical symptoms may need a treatment regimen that is rooted in emotional restoration and healing. After a lifetime of counseling others, the wounded healer may need to seek counsel for his or her emotional distress.

"I can talk about it without having those physical issues now," Mike says slowly. "I can talk about it without picking up all of the tension and all of the pain. I can talk about it without getting all stirred up over the unfairness of everything."

He pauses, deep in his thoughts.

"Unfairness.

"That word—unfairness—is what I would probably use for a headline, if I were writing the story of what happened to me. If I had made some great mistake, like having an affair with my secretary or preaching a false gospel or something, then what happened to me might make sense. It would still be a sad story, but I would be able to point back to the 'why' it happened. I could tell myself that what happened was unfortunate, but it was set up and triggered by something I had done. Something stupid. Something immoral. If there were a big mistake or a big error on my part, I would own it. In fact, it would help the story make sense in a way that, frankly, it just doesn't.

"As it is, if I were writing my story of what did happen, I wouldn't try to paint myself as a hero or claim that I was ever a superpastor or try to make myself look better than I was—or better than I am. I know I'm not a Rick Warren or a Joel Osteen or a Bill Hybels. I understand that. God created those guys for a certain type of service and prominence, and he obviously made me for other kinds of uses. I've never had a problem with that idea. I've never had delusions of grandeur. I think my self-image is fairly healthy and reasonably accurate overall.

"I wouldn't even try to claim that I was an excellent pastor or the best pastor in that church's overall history. But what I would tell you is what is absolutely true. I loved God, I loved my family, and I totally loved being the pastor of that church. I was doing the best I knew how, and my ministry was bearing fruit.

"The church was growing, the board was happy with me, and we were reaching new people and new families for Christ. I could sit down in my office and count up the families and the people who were new to our church—and many of them also new to Jesus—during my time in ministry there.

"Things were going well. Anyone would have told you that. I could see myself having a long-term ministry there. I could see my wife and my kids living in the same house, in the same town, for a very long time. I sometimes thought about retiring into that setting—that's how well things were going. When things are good, a minister doesn't think about moving up or moving out. I was ready to stay forever.

"Then out of nowhere, for no reason at all, everything changed."

Moments later Mike adds this coda to his existing remarks.

"I didn't deserve what happened to me.

"Nobody deserves to have that happen to them."

We've scheduled only one hour for this specific encounter with an ex-pastor, but more than two hours later we are still sitting there in the same Starbucks. We've gone back through the line a second time, picking up three slices of pumpkin bread because all three of us are hungry. Mike has talked us through his pastoral exodus from every angle, especially focusing on the impact it had on his family. He shows no signs of carrying a grudge or being bitter about the end results of the conflict. He talks calmly and naturally. If anything, in our view, he may be too hard on himself as he reviews everyone's conduct—including his own—during the season that led up to the end of his ministry at a medium-sized church.

He is quick to point out his own shortcomings, but he is more gracious in describing the role that others played. There is no one person that he singles out as an enemy—no harmful person that he blames for what happened to him. Meanwhile, the story itself continues to unfold.

"I was accused of heresy," he tells us fairly early in the interview. "Not in those words, because outside of seminary I don't know anyone who actually uses the word 'heresy.' But I was accused of being unfaithful to the doctrine of our church. I was accused of failing to preach our doctrine often enough or well enough, and also I was accused of preaching ideas that were directly in conflict with our beliefs.

"None of those charges were true—not in any way," Mike insists. "You don't have to like me and you don't have to like my family. You don't have to like how I look or how I talk. You don't have to like my wife or my family. Liking someone is a very personal decision. I've gotten used to the fact that some people just don't like me, and they aren't going to like me no matter what I do!

"But it's one thing to not like me—which is okay—and it's another thing altogether to make up false charges against me, just to get rid of me. And that is exactly what happened to me. A few people in the church got upset, for reasons I still don't know and may never know. They decided that the church would be better off if I wasn't the pastor. They used lies and rumors and misinformation to get things so stirred up that I don't think Jesus could have kept his job as their pastor!"

Mike is silent for a moment.

"I have never preached against the doctrines of our church," he says slowly and with careful emphasis. "In fact, the two sermons that seemed to get me into the most trouble were almost exact copies of sermons that one of my professors in seminary preached to us. That professor went on to hold the highest office in our denomination! That professor wrote books about this particular subject. And my sermons used his same outlines. I just changed the stories and illustrations and used his same ideas and concepts. The two sermons that basically ended my career were both from sermons he preached and from ideas he used in his books.

"If he had been serving here as their pastor, would they have accused *him* of preaching heresy?" Mike wonders aloud.

"Would they have tried so hard to get *him* to leave the church?"

All of us are silent for a few minutes.

"I went to our denomination's seminary," Mike asserts. "I graduated with honors from that school. I took two classes that studied the theological issue these people were accusing me about. No offense, but I was the one who knew what I was talking about—they weren't. I was the one who was being faithful to the core doctrines of our Zion—they weren't. I was the one who wanted to preach and teach and expand that core doctrine, not hide it away out of sight.

"But it really wasn't about any of that," Mike insists. "They used the whole doctrine thing as a weapon to get me to leave. But it wasn't about that. They just wanted to get rid of me and put a different pastor in there. And I still don't know why! I don't know what the real reason was. Maybe I never will."

Caught in the crosshairs of sudden and seemingly baseless attacks, Mike hoped for support and comfort from among his board members and key leaders. Yet as is so often the case, these leaders at first ignored the attacks. Later, as the attacks grew impossible to ignore, the board members and key leaders minimized the importance of the conflict. Even after the problem emerged into full view, these leaders were reluctant to confront Mike's attackers or defuse the tension.

Mike believed—accurately so—that he had the full support of his board, his staff, and the leaders of various volunteer ministries. Yet somehow this support, which was tangible and real, failed to materialize as any kind of political help or strategic counsel during the most difficult battle of Mike's ministerial life.

One board member, who had become a very close friend, did eventually attempt to wade into the fray, aligning himself as Mike's supporter. However, by the time this assistance was finally offered, the battle was mostly over. By the time this particular board member stood up to be counted, the fighting was mostly finished—and Mike's exit from the pastorate was virtually assured.

"I'm truly grateful that he stood up for me," Mike assures us. "I really am. But, honestly, there was a very long time where no one was sticking up for me, at least not publicly and not out loud. I kept hoping for someone—at least one voice—to just speak up and tell the world that these attacks on me were untrue, unfair, and way out of line.

"I kept hoping for somebody—anybody—to have my back, but when it finally did happen it was way too late. It was like when a football team is losing a big game by a whole lot of points. At the very last minute they rush down the field and score a meaningless touchdown, after which they still lose the big game.

"Are you supposed to cheer for the touchdown when that happens? I mean, they've already lost. The outcome is still the outcome.

"By the time this guy found his voice and stood up for me, the battle was already over. He meant well, but everything had gone way too far by then."

Mike's voice trails off into silence.

"It was nice of him, but it wasn't enough, and it didn't come soon enough."

This theme—help from key leaders coming along as too little, too late is one that we'll hear from several former pastors we interview for our book.

When Others Are Hurting Too

We hear a similar narrative from a Canadian pastor several months later. Besieged by critics on every side and feeling afraid to defend himself for fear of appearing defensive or hostile, this hardworking and highly ethical pastor relied on the aid of the members of the elder board. Instead of defending himself and facing his attackers, the pastor busied himself with preaching, teaching, and calling on his constituents—the core duties of his essential role as a minister. He worked harder on his sermons than ever before. He called on more people, more often, than ever before. He was over-performing—a common response to ungrounded criticism or unexpected conflict in the church.

Meanwhile, the continuing attacks on this pastor and his ministry, which were groundless and without any foundation in fact or reality, were coming from a small but committed group of upset people, some of whom were not even regular attenders of the church. Relentlessly this small group was making their claims, spreading their gossip, and doing everything in their power to make the pastor's life difficult or impossible. Clearly their goal was to get rid of the pastor and start over. To a lesser extent, this group of malcontents may have been trying to somehow take over the church or at least to grab a disproportionate share of the power and resources of the church. They were outsiders who were perhaps hoping to become insiders or to tip the balance of political power in their own favor. Some had long since left for other congregations in other parts of town, but now here they were, stirring up problems for a dedicated young pastor.

Against such a coordinated and relentless assault on his own integrity and his approach to ministry, the pastor felt like he should leave the fighting to others rather than seeming to defend himself. After all, weren't the claims utterly false? Wouldn't anyone who checked on the situation discover the truth—which totally validated the pastor and his ministry?

"I was letting our elder board deal with it," this Canadian pastor relates. "There was no truth to any of the rumors about me that were swirling around. Overall it seemed wiser to let the elder board step up and do their job—be the spiritual leaders they were elected to be. Even when things were fairly intense, this seemed like something they could handle.

"But what I didn't notice was the toll it was taking on all of them as a group and on one of the men in particular. He had been my ally and my friend all the way through these things. He and I had a really good relationship. I had been there for his family during some tough times. Now he was being there for me.

"We were standing in the church hallway one day after a meeting. We were actually talking about something else, not about all of these problems. On a whim I just turned to him and asked him how he was doing. His response shocked me completely.

"He looked at me and said, 'Well, I wake up with panic attacks, I have dizzy spells several times a day, and during the average day I break down crying three or four times.'"

Our pastor friend is silent, remembering the moment as an epiphany.

"I just stood there, so surprised by what I was hearing. In all this time I had never asked the guy how *he* was doing. Up until that point, everything had been about how I was doing under the stress of all the attacks.

"Later in our conversation he told me that his four-year-old daughter had recently asked her mother one night before her bedtime, 'Why isn't Daddy ever happy anymore?'"

The pastor pauses his narrative once again.

"When he told me that, I just lost it. My heart totally went out to him. Up until that moment I had been focused on the damage to me, the damage to my wife and my family. I hadn't even noticed how much the key leaders and board members were also suffering, how much tension and stress they were under.

"Until that moment, and before that conversation in the church hallway, I hadn't understood that there were other people who were hurting in all of that. And some of them were my strongest supporters in the church."

This story and Mike's story from earlier in this chapter combine to paint nearly identical pictures of a committed and caring pastor who is under duress, while those who defend him are also beset with much anxiety. Some exhibit the physical symptoms that typify and characterize a high-stress environment—lack of sleep, frequent colds or other illnesses, and a range of anxiety-related disorders.

"It had taken me a while to convince people to even serve on the board," the Canadian pastor tells us at one point in our interview. "I mean, I really had to recruit people aggressively. I really had to convince them to serve. Once they got there, they were doing a pretty good job of helping to prayerfully guide our church.

"But nothing in their training or background prepared any of them to support or defend a pastor who is suddenly under attack. We don't have a manual for that! We don't have a guidebook for lay leaders of congregations, helping them know how to defuse conflict or when to call in some reinforcements from outside of the context and the setting.

"My board did the best they could, they really did," admits the Canadian pastor. "But it just wasn't in their nature to go up against a determined, relentless group of people who were persecuting me. In general the women and men on my board wanted to *avoid* conflict, not wade into the midst of it and settle things. They weren't trained to deal with problems like that, and it wasn't in their personalities to be so confrontational and so assertive. They were polite, well-mannered people who just didn't know how to handle trouble while it was unfolding all around them.

"I was proud of them before all the trouble happened, and I still am proud of them as I look back at their service to the church. When I was forced out, about half of them resigned from the board immediately. Most of the rest of them found a way to leave the board over the next few weeks and months.

"Some of my board members ended up leaving that church. I had nothing to do with their decisions. I stayed away from all of that, and I am still staying away. But I heard later that some of my key board members left the church and went to other places. After all they had seen, they didn't want to keep on attending a church like that, a church that would treat a pastor in such a harmful and unfair way. They didn't want their kids growing up in that kind of an environment, either.

"Would you want *your* kids to grow up in a church like that?" the former pastor wonders aloud.

It's a relevant and perceptive question.

Is There Any Help from Above?

Another common theme that emerged in interviews with ex-pastors is the lament that when they needed help and support from above, it somehow never materialized. By "help from above" they are not referring to divine intervention but to assistance from denominational superiors such as bishops and superintendents.

"I called my D.S. [district superintendent] the minute things flared up," says one former pastor during our interview with him. "I felt like he needed to know, and I also hoped he would show up at the church, confront the problem people, and bring all the conflict to healthy resolution.

"I know that's not realistic," the ex-pastor admits, "but that's how I felt. In that moment of battle, with so much pressure bearing down on me and my family, I felt like my D.S. was the one person in the world who could and should come riding to my rescue.

"I didn't know him real well before that," he continues, "but I thought we were friends. I thought he had my back. As it was, he listened to me very politely but he didn't have any specific advice to offer. He didn't come out to our church and look around. I called him a few more times while everything was going on, but I gradually realized that help—at least help from him—just wasn't on the way."

We hear versions of the same opinion from others who left the ministry after experiences of conflict and difficulty in their congregations. Some of these former pastors exhibit reactions of bitterness or anger; others are more resigned in their acceptance of a rescue that never happened or of help that was never offered.

In a candid conversation with an experienced superintendent, we raise the question of how to support pastors when they are mired in conflict. The response we receive is both wise and insightful.

"In our tradition, people get elected to the superintendency," our guest says as we begin. "They don't graduate from superintendent school and then submit applications to serve. They aren't interviewed and tested by the human resources department to see how well they know the landscape of the superintendency.

"They get elected. Sometimes they are a missionary coming home from being overseas. Sometimes they are a pastor from a prominent church on the district that is electing them. Sometimes they are a person who has grown up in that area or on that district, and the election is kind of a homecoming experience.

"But my point is simple," the leader continues. "Although we do offer some orientation and training for our superintendents, most of them tend to get their training on-the-job, rather than before-the-job. You can't possibly understand what a major difference that makes until you're out in the field, watching the results."

Later in the same interview our guest offers another reaction to the same overall question how—and how much—should pastors be supported when there is open conflict between the pastor and the congregation.

"This may not be the answer you are looking for," our guest tells us. "But here's how it is. The superintendent may realize that after the conflict, when all is said and done, the church will still be there. The pastor may be gone. The pastor may be serving on another district somewhere. But the church will still be there, and the lay leaders of the church will still be there.

"I am not trying to justify anything or to speak for all superintendents. I am just trying to point out one dynamic of the situation. The superintendent knows that after the battle, no matter how things work out, the church will still be there, and the people of the church will still be there.

"Sometimes maybe it seems like the superintendent sides with the church, and if so, maybe the superintendent is just caring for the flock that he knows will still be a part of his flock after the conflict is over. The men and women who remain on that district, year after year, are the ones the superintendent will be dealing with later. So perhaps, and again I am not speaking for others, perhaps sometimes the superintendent may tend to focus on the longer term. After the dust settles, who will still be around? Who will still be on this district?"

These are salient and compelling issues.

The role of the superintendency is an inviting topic for another book.

Pastors who leave the ministry often believe that their denominational supervisor could have—or should have—done more to help the pastor keep his or her job. Many of these former ministers believe that their situations might have ended differently if only the bishop or superintendent had intervened in the matter or intervened earlier.

Many believe that the superintendent (in their opinion) should enter the situation with objectivity and with basic fairness, much like a referee functions in boxing, basketball, or other venues. Others believe that a superintendent should always support his or her pastors, no matter what. "If you're not going to support your pastors when they need you," one ex-minister asks rhetorically, "then what's the point? Either you're there for them or you're not."

When a pastor and a congregation are in conflict, the situation is not unlike a minefield littered with buried explosives. It's not difficult to understand why a person serving as superintendent, who is coming in from the outside, may step lightly, not wanting to detonate an explosive. Those in denominational office may tend to move more slowly, act more carefully, and exercise more restraint than we might wish for, particularly if we are a pastor under siege. But if we can back away from our own specific problems for a moment, long enough to look at the big picture, we can see why caution is so often a wise approach.

Although this is an anecdotal observation and not a scholastic thesis, please briefly consider the following proposition: In general, fiery and hot-tempered leaders do not tend to be elected to positions as bishops or superintendents. The ones who successfully climb the ecclesiastical ladder are more likely to think first, act slowly, and move forward with caution. Whether this is a matter of temperament, a function of maturity, or simply a strategic calculation, the calm and the cautious advance.

In the midst of a flaming conflict, it may be disappointing to be served by a cautious person who does not seem to have your back. However, it is a realistic and reasonable expectation to believe that your denominational superior will move slowly, think carefully, and act with caution when he or she arrives on the scene.

Do you find it so?

Questions for Reflection

Pastors and Ministers

1. We interviewed a number of pastors who reported the same cluster of physical symptoms during or after intense church conflict. Have you experienced any of these physical symptoms as a response to stress or conflict while serving as the pastor of a local church? In whom (if anyone) did you confide about the nature and extent of your physical health struggles during a conflict?

2. Mike's board finally supported him, but it was too little, too late. Mike is not bitter as he reflects on this, but if you were Mike, might you be bitter, angry, or at least disappointed in your board and leaders? Do you expect them to defend you promptly, honestly, and well? What is the expectation that you have of your board and leaders when you are wrongly accused or attacked by a critic?

3. The Canadian pastor we discussed in this chapter had a very supportive board. They swung into action but perhaps because these leaders were too polite or too nice, the noisy critics were winning the battles and eventually won the war. Does this outcome seem inevitable to you? In a case where the church board actually has your back, do you believe that they will eventually prevail in their struggle, win the battle, and defend the truth?

4. Point blank: Should a denominational leader of your region have your back? Should you be automatically protected and defended by him or her? Why or why not? Thinking about your current superintendent, do you honestly believe that he or she would defend you in a crisis? Can you count on that person to believe you, to trust you, and to support you? Why or why not?

5. If you believed that continuing to serve in pastoral ministry was destroying your physical or emotional health, would you continue to fight the good fight, or would you rush for the exit? Would you prefer to stay in the heat of the battle or to get away, recover from your wounds, and live again to fight another day in some other setting? Which outcome seems the most noble or admirable? Which choice would you be more likely to make if you were suffering during a conflict?

Local Churches and Church Boards

1. When there is conflict involving a pastor and the congregation, should the local congregation solve its own problems or should an outside authority enter the situation and serve as a referee of sorts? At what point, if any, should an outside authority enter a conflicted congregation in order to help bring a positive resolution? Should this authority be called in or should it simply show up and attempt to take control of a bad situation? How much actual authority should this outside party or person have in resolving the difficult church conflict? Or should the local congregation have and hold full authority over its own conflicts and over the matter of how to resolve them?

2. In Mike's case, board members were slow to realize the intensity and the determination of the pastor's critics. The board members were passive and slow to react, choosing a strategy of hoping for the best. Not surprisingly, the conflict was already way out of control by the time one of the pastor's friends on the board finally stood up to be counted and to support the pastor. Could this kind of disaster happen in your church? Why or why not? Does your board tend to be passive and subdued in the face of attacks and criticisms, or do they powerfully and immediately respond to any and all attacks on your pastor? What typifies your board's response to conflict?

3. If a denominational leader is called in to mediate conflict in your church, do you assume or expect that this leader will be likely to support the pastor's perspective, or to take the church's side in the matter? All other things being equal, do you expect the denominational leader to think like a clergyperson, to automatically defend the clergyperson, or do you expect the outside (and above) denominational leader to intervene on behalf of the church, in order to "protect" the congregation from the pastor? Whose side is the denominational leader going to be on? What do you expect from the denominational leader who is called in to help your church manage conflict?

4. How many pastors do you know who have left a congregation after, or due to, conflict and struggles in the church? How many former pastors of your own local congregation have left your church for reasons like this? How likely is it that your current or future pastor will face destructive conflict within the local church where you serve and lead? What are you doing to prevent this from happening or to be prepared when conflict arises?

5. To what extent, if any, do you believe that you are personally objective and open-minded with regard to any division or struggle between a church and its pastor?

Denominational Leaders

1. Some former superintendents told us that the role of a denominational leader sometimes goes to a person without the experience and training that is needed. Do you find it so? Does this seem to be one reasonable explanation as to why superintendents are not always active and visibly engaged in protecting their pastors during a conflict?

2. Another perspective we received from superintendents involved the time frame of "after the battle is over." The reality of the situa-

tion is that when the battle ends, the church and its lay leaders will still be on the district, while the specific individual pastor may leave the church and/or leave the district. According to this rationale, the superintendent may consciously or unconsciously side with the constituents who are the most likely to remain on his or her district—within his or her territory and responsibility—after the battle. Do you agree with this perspective in any way? If so, does it help to explain why a superintendent may appear to not "have the back" of his or her pastor(s) in a given situation of conflict or disagreement?

3. When a pastor on your district is undergoing intense stress, to the point of experiencing physical symptoms, are you likely to know about it? Are your pastors likely to confide in you if they are suffering in this way? Why or why not? To what extent do you proactively reach out to pastors in order to gauge or assess their emotional health and physical wellness?

4. When a pastor asks you for help with a congregational conflict, to what extent are you personally likely to "side with the pastor" in any dispute? Before you know the facts of the specific case and the contours of the specific situation, are you more likely to defend the pastor or to protect the congregation? Which is your natural first response?

5. To what extent, if any, does anxiety about your own political career or personal popularity impact your response to a church in crisis? To what extent, if any, does "protecting yourself" impact your supervision of and your ministry to a church that is in crisis or a pastor who is embattled?

6. Do you feel supported by a higher authority (denominationally speaking) when you enter into a situation of conflict in an attempt to mediate? Do you feel unprotected and vulnerable, or do you believe

that someone higher on the denominational ladder can, does, or will support you if needed?

FOUR

PROPHETS, PRIESTS, AND KINGS

POWER, CONTROL, AND EXPECTATIONS IN MINISTRY

With Janet's mom arriving to stay the weekend as their sitter, Mark and Janet left their kids at home with Grandma, driving 350 miles to interview at a new church. Mark had arranged for a few days of much-needed vacation time at his current church; no one suspected he was using his vacation to pursue another job.

The drive to a prosperous suburb of a large city in the South took Mark and Janet through some of the most beautiful scenery in the country, in their opinion. There were lush fields and verdant green valleys, interrupted by rolling hills and acres of forests spreading out as far as the eye could see. By the time they arrived, both Mark and Janet were already feeling more relaxed and at ease. For a weekend at least, they would escape the tensions of pastoral ministry. Although Mark recalls feeling a bit "keyed up" (but not nervous, he assures us) before the interview, both Mark and Janet were excited, hoping for a positive outcome.

Mark's interview with the church board would occur on Saturday morning, after which he would then be preaching a sermon on Sunday morning. In advance of those two main events, the prospective pastoral couple was scheduled to arrive at the church on a Friday afternoon. There they would meet a board member who would take them to dinner and get them settled into their local hotel. This part of the weekend was not official—they would not be meeting the board, they would not be interviewed—they would simply be having dinner and getting their motel keys.

Since the Friday evening meal time was not a part of their "official" itinerary, both Mark and Janet felt comfortable traveling in casual clothes. Mark was in jeans and a T-shirt. Janet was wearing her favorite pair of jeans with a light sweater. Between the comfort of their casual attire and the beauty of the scenery they were driving through, both Mark and Janet greatly enjoyed their trip. They didn't feel sloppy or worry about looking scruffy—until they arrived at the church.

Standing beside a dark Mercedes in the parking lot was an impeccably dressed middle-aged man in a suit and tie. He was not quite old enough to be the age of their parents, but close. As Mark drove his aging Taurus into the lot, he had his first pang of anxiety about Friday night's non-official schedule. He had been told that dinner would be simple, quick, and casual—not exactly a suit-and-Mercedes occasion! Suddenly it appeared that both he and Janet were underdressed for the evening. Just as suddenly, it felt like their car was the oldest and least maintained on the planet. "I was planning to wash my car on Saturday, after we got down there," Mark recalls, "since it would just get dirty on the long drive anyway."

"Even my shoes betrayed me," Mark recalls. "I was wearing my favorite pair of old Nikes. The guy who met us was wearing shoes that probably cost more than I made in a week at the church I was serving."

Despite the evident disparity in appearance, their waiting host immediately put them at ease with his broad smile and bright charm. "Welcome!" he said, reaching out his arms to embrace both Mark and Janet. "We're so glad you could be with us this weekend!"

Moments later, the young pastoral couple was riding to dinner in an S-class, leaving their car behind at the church. Their new host was driving, and at the host's insistence Mark was sitting up in front. Janet, stretched out in regal comfort in the backseat, felt like she was riding along in a chauffeured limousine.

"They ignored me for the whole drive over to dinner," is how Janet recalls that portion of the evening. "[Our host] was talking to Mark the whole time, firing a bunch of questions at him."

Their host took Mark and Janet to a fancy restaurant in an upscale neighborhood. There was a table reserved for them; it appeared that their companion was a regular customer. The servers seemed visibly excited to see him arrive, and no one appeared to be disturbed by Mark and Janet's casual clothing. No one, that is, except Mark and Janet, both of whom were feeling underdressed and unprepared for the kind of evening that was unfolding.

"I remember thinking it was odd that [his] wife wasn't with us," Janet says in looking back on that fateful Friday. "It was just him, no wife or kids, no one else from the church. He ushered us into that restaurant and people started rushing to serve him. All three of us had menus in our hands, ice water in our glasses, and a carafe of coffee set out on our table, before we could even sit down."

Both Mark and Janet recall the excellence of the meal itself.

"I was trying not to notice the prices," Mark grins. "But I couldn't help myself. Before I knew what was happening, he had talked me into a side order of some kind of macaroni and cheese that had ham in it. And I happened to glance at that part of the menu—my side order was $8 or $9!"

Unaccustomed to $40 steaks and $9 sides, Mark and Janet both attempted to order something cheap from the menu, only to have their companion insist that they follow his lead and try some of the house favorites.

"I don't know what our total restaurant bill was that night," Mark sighs, "but I'm guessing it was well over $200 and probably closer to $300—for only three people! For Janet and me, it was the first time in our lives we had dined at that level."

Meanwhile, their host was charming, genial, and full of stories.

"He kept us laughing all through the meal," Janet remembers. "Mark and I didn't have to say very much. We mostly just nodded our heads and enjoyed the food."

During the meal, their host did manage to convey some news about the hiring salary range that the church would be offering. The base pay was double what Mark was making at the time, plus came with a list of perks that seemed a mile long.

"I didn't want to make my decision based on the money," Mark insists. "That's not my true value system. But honestly once he brought up the salary amount plus the allowances and the benefits and the total package, I couldn't quit thinking about how much better off my family would be, if somehow I got this job."

As the meal concluded their host drove them back to the church parking lot, reached into his pocket, and pulled out two card keys to a room at a nearby all-suite hotel. "We passed this place about a mile back. You probably noticed it," he told the couple. "You're already checked in; don't worry about a thing. We'll see you at 10 a.m. right back here at the church for the first phase of your interview!"

As they unlocked the doors of their car, their aging Taurus felt older and looked grubbier than they remembered it. Their clothes felt more worn out, and both Mark and Janet felt poor.

"We were actually doing okay at the time," Mark admits. "We didn't walk around feeling sorry for ourselves or thinking we were poor people. But that night as we got back to our car to drive over to the hotel, suddenly our clothes and our car felt old and worn out. And we felt like a couple of poor people who had somehow arrived in the land of the rich."

Somewhat intimidated by the wardrobe of their host, Mark and Janet decided they would shop for clothes the next afternoon, during their few available hours of free time during the interview weekend. Both of them bought new shoes; at Janet's insistence Mark bought a new tie to wear for his Sunday morning message.

Saturday's interview went well, Sunday's message went well, and by the time they climbed back into their aging Taurus to drive home, both Mark and Janet were feeling cautiously optimistic about their chances of getting the job. When the phone rang on the following Thursday morning, they were elated to learn that the board had unanimously voted to offer them the pastorate. By denominational polity the next step would be a congregational vote, scheduled for two weeks from Sunday.

"We were so nervous that whole time, waiting for that vote," Janet admits. "We couldn't tell anybody that we had interviewed there. Only my mom and dad knew, plus Mark's stepmom. Our kids knew but they were young at the time and we had sworn them to secrecy. As far as I know, they didn't reveal our secret."

Two weeks from that Sunday, the church voted very positively to invite Mark to be their next pastor. The margin of the vote was overwhelming, and Mark and Janet needed no other confirmation that this move was God's will for their lives. They said yes to the move and began to make plans accordingly.

Peering Back into the Foreshadows

The next few weeks rushed by in a flurry of packing and good-byes. Mark announced his resignation to a stunned church board, then to a suddenly quiet congregation. Both announcements were difficult.

"We had no idea you were thinking of leaving," one friend and board member said to Mark and Janet. "If we had known this, we would have done anything we could to help you decide to stay."

Other members of the congregation were effusive in their praise and also visibly sorry to see the young couple depart for another assignment. All of these reactions, while they may seem like a normal aspect of many pastoral transitions, caught Mark and Janet by surprise.

"I had no idea we were so loved there," Janet explains. "I was proud of Mark for the great job he was doing as their pastor, but it's not like we were getting a lot of compliments or we heard a lot of positive feedback.

"For the most part, people didn't say anything at all. They weren't attacking us, but they weren't usually praising us either. We had no idea how they really felt while we served there. Things were normal, not exceptional. People were nice, but they didn't express much praise or much support.

"All of a sudden, after we announced we were leaving, it seemed like everyone in the church loved us dearly, like they really admired Mark as a pastor, and it seemed like all of them wanted us to stay."

Janet is quiet, remembering the season.

"Even though we were really excited about our move," she tells us, "it ended up being really hard to leave [name of church]. There was just a huge outpouring of love and affection for us. People were giving us gifts, taking us out to dinner, and treating us better than we had been treated the whole time we served there.

"They had been treating us just fine—I'm not saying things were bad before. But all of a sudden everyone kind of dialed it up a notch and we felt more loved, more respected, and more valued than we had ever felt when we were busy serving them in ministry.

"I remember lying awake one night before the move," Janet sighs. "I was thinking, 'I sure hope we're doing the right thing! Because these people in our current church seem to genuinely, truly love us!'"

Regardless of the warmth of their departure, Mark and Janet had made their decision and felt locked in to accept the new call. They packed and planned and made the move, trying not to notice the sad faces sprinkled throughout the congregation they were leaving behind.

A royal welcome at their new church helped ease the fears of the young couple. A generous moving allowance had arrived well in advance of their trip, allowing the family to dine out, stay in a hotel for one night, and generally enjoy the trip as a family excursion. Their new church owned a parsonage—an idea that seemed like a remnant from a bygone era. Yet it allowed the move to be simpler.

There were no rental houses to tour. There was no Realtor to show them around looking at houses to purchase. Instead there was a large, sprawling parsonage to move into, located near, but not too near, the campus of the church they would be serving.

As they unlocked the door of the parsonage and began moving in, Mark found two paychecks waiting for him on a countertop in the kitchen area: one for salary and one for housing allowance. Even though he knew exactly what he would be paid, the size of the checks caused Mark to audibly gasp. The move was becoming real, and the new reality seemed pleasant.

Three months later, Mark's view of his new role had changed dramatically. Attendance was up, giving was up, and the arrival of a new senior minister was giving the congregation a positive bounce that was delighting almost everyone—except the pastor himself.

The prevailing morale in the church was tangibly upbeat; Mark and Janet were being treated well and received warmly by everyone.

Yet while living in a parsonage with more than enough room for his family, and while happily cashing paychecks that were outsized compared with any prior season in his ministerial life, Mark found himself becoming restless and ill at ease. He had trouble sleeping at night. He worried that he had made the wrong decision or that he had made his decision for the wrong reasons.

"It took me about three months, but it became very apparent to me as I settled in down there," Mark says now. "I had fallen into a classic honey trap. The more I looked around at my new setting, the more I realized that I might have seen this coming in advance. I should have picked up on the clues that were out there, even before I finished my original interview."

At Mark's new church, the same gentleman who had welcomed him for the interview, escorting Mark and his wife for an evening of fine dining, was also the person who set the tone, established the priorities, and determined the direction of the church as a whole. With a warm smile, a gracious Southern manner, and the charm of a practiced politician, this man held absolute sway over the decisions and dimensions of church life. Or to put it another way, the man who held the keys to the shiny Mercedes clearly held the keys to the church also.

"He was not an evil person," Mark insists. "He did not act in bad faith. On the contrary, he was—and is today—the very description of the word 'gentleman.' He can be one of the nicest, most charming people you have ever met! But under that exterior of smiles and warmth is a shrewd, calculating, experienced businessman.

"He is far wealthier than I realized at first," Mark sighs. "I mean, I've known people who drove Mercedes that they couldn't really afford. I've known people who would take you out to dinner to show you how prosperous they were, while they were living on credit card debt and little else.

"This guy is just the opposite. Beyond the flashy car and the expensive meals and the huge—I mean enormous—house he lives in, this guy has more wealth than meets the eye. He owns buildings and businesses all over town. He has property in South America, Hawaii, and other places. I don't know the full scope of his holdings, but I know he is far wealthier than his friends at church realize.

"Did I mention that he's a nice guy?" Mark's face relaxes into a smile.

"He truly is. I also think he means well, in general. He functions every day in a world in which there is only one ruler—himself. And when he steps into the church he expects the church world to defer to and honor him in the same way that his broader environment always serves him.

"Honestly, it happens just as he wishes it would. The church treats him the same way the servers and waiters did at the [restaurant] when he took us to dinner. Everyone wants to be sure that he is happy, that he is on board with something, that anything and everything we do has his support behind it. It's not a written policy anywhere, but it doesn't need to be. For at least a decade and probably more, there has been one person setting the pace for that church.

"If something does not have his support behind it, forget it," Mark says, shaking his head slowly. "Once again, I have to tell you—this is not an evil person. This is a really good guy. But he has held so much power for so long, maybe even he does not realize how much influence and control he ends up having."

Mark and Janet stayed at their new church for nearly three years. Mark's tenure there was a positive, upward, steadily-growing season for the congregation. Just before the three-year anniversary of Mark's pastorate, he prayed and accepted a management role at a missions organization based in another state.

"We downsized our house, we scaled back our lifestyle, and we definitely moved in a downward motion financially as well as geographically," Mark tells us today. "In financial terms, maybe our move didn't make sense to other people. Maybe they wondered about us, or wondered what I was thinking.

"But at the end of the day, I get to both serve and lead here at [name of missions organization]. There is a group of us here who all have senior roles in the leadership. We meet together for group prayer and discussion several times a week. We try to move in alignment with what the Holy Spirit is telling us to do.

"We're not perfect here—none of us are. But this group moves with such a spiritual process and such a lack of ego. This place has been absolutely refreshing to me, like an oasis in the desert. After watching one man control a whole church, I am now watching God work through a praying, unified group of leaders who control a missionary movement that is spreading around the world."

Mark finishes his story.

"I am so much happier here than I ever was anywhere else," he tells us. "Being around this kind of process, sharing leadership with this caliber of other guys, all of this is really a blessing to be a part of.

"I'd have more money saved up if I had stayed there and pastored longer," Mark says of his previous assignment. "But money can't buy what I have here. I get to watch God work, see what God is doing, and be a part of the broader reach of God into unreached people groups every day.

"Frankly, if I could afford it, I would do this job for free."

Prophets, Priests, and Kings

As we researched and wrote our book *Managing Stress in Ministry*, we interviewed many working ministers who described their frustrations with the unique ambiguities inherent in the role of pastor.

A look at the major stressors of pastoral life finds "role ambiguity" at or near the top of most lists. In contrast to a well-defined position at the bottom or the top of the food chain, the role of pastor is rife with internal contradictions and seemingly irreconcilable differences in its level of authority.

On the one hand, a pastor is expected to function as a visible and effective leader. Within a larger church context, a pastor's leadership skills may be almost as important as his or her preaching and teaching ability. Yet in many pastoral contexts, the same pastor who functions as the leader is also a paid employee of a church, with most churches expressing their authority over the pastor through the use of a church board that controls pastoral pay, the working conditions in which the pastor functions, and many other aspects of the pastoral environment.

So at one and the same time, a pastor is seen as the leader of a religious organization, while on the other hand he or she is a mere functionary, receiving a weekly or monthly paycheck in exchange for services rendered. Inherent in this ambiguous role is a vaunted position as leader and a subservient and perhaps demeaning role as a "mere employee" who serves at the whim of the board.

Against this backdrop it may be helpful to consider some of the biblical types of leadership and the ways in which these types may be expected of pastors in the context of their ministry assignments. Among these are prophet, priest, and king.

Prophet

We are not talking here of a formal spiritual gifting for prophecy, or of the phenomenon called "a word of knowledge" in many settings. Instead we are talking here about a role, not an experience.

The role of prophet is one of exhortation, calling a group of people or perhaps a whole nation to look at God, to pay attention to God, to hear God's voice, and to receive God's instruction.

There is a prophet element woven into the tapestry of the pastoral robe. Pastors are expected to preach and teach God's word and his precepts, thus exhorting the congregation to more faithfully follow God's ways. Ministers may have greater or lesser gifts in this exhortation role, but it is expected of a minister that he or she will be able to faithfully preach and proclaim God's Word, calling the faithful to obedience and service.

In almost every congregation, pastors are expected to be the primary prophets and exhorters. This role may be shared among a team of teaching or preaching pastors, yet the role is expected of each member of the team. In smaller settings with only one pastor, that person is expected to be the preacher, teacher, and exhorter. Many church boards and congregations, if asked to name their top priority in finding a new minister, will simply declare "find us a good preacher."

Although there are layers of meaning wrapped into that instruction, the primary thrust of it is clear: Find us someone who can faithfully preach and proclaim God's Word to us and to the lost in our community. This prophetic role of pastoral ministry is front and center in the expectations of most congregations and most leader boards. This prophetic role often provides the template against which the success or effectiveness of a minister will be measured and evaluated.

No minister can do everything well, but most ministers are expected to have a level of gifts and graces for serving the role of prophet, teacher, exhorter, and proclaimer of God's Holy Word. If the pastoral role were mostly or entirely prophetic in nature, there would be far less ambiguity dotting the landscape of parish ministry.

Yet as it is, there are several more dimensions of expectations. Beyond being a prophet and teacher, a minister may be expected to have other skill sets. He or she may be expected to serve in other key functions and aspects of ministry that—although not as central as the prophetic role—are part and parcel of the expressed or implied job description.

Priest

If the prophetic role is one of exhorter, then the priestly role is one of intercessor. Although this specific role does not always appear in the explicit and formal job description of a minister, it is usually held as a tacit and quietly understood priority. The pastor is regarded as someone who will intercede on behalf of the church, its people, and its needs.

The local church pastor is expected to be a person of prayer. He or she is expected to have an active, vital prayer life that serves as a point of connection to God. In this way the pastor is both intercessor and also to some extent an intermediary, and here we get into theological danger very quickly. Most of us believe in something called the priesthood of all believers, so let's not argue here. But perhaps we can admit that there is often a commonly held assumption within a church that the pastor is close to God—or at least is a lot closer to God than a "normal" person. So if you want to have something prayed about and you want the prayers to reach God, you call on the pastor to pray because after all, he or she is a professional religious person and is closer to God. And in that sense, via folk theology, we can see how the pastor might function as an intermediary, despite the best of intentions.

Can we quit worrying about the theological implications for a moment and just consider the practical matters? Jesus is the high priest for us all. We now have through Christ the only priest we will ever need (see Hebrews 7 for a fuller discussion here). Christ alone is our one true priest, and under his lordship those of us who follow him share in a universal priesthood of all believers.

In spite of these verities, it is not uncommon for the members of a church to look to their pastor for spiritual services, including intercessory prayer. It is not rare for someone who is sick to call for the pastor to come and visit so that the pastor can pray. We can disagree with this theologically all we want to, but meanwhile the practical reality is still right there, staring us all in the face.

We can strategically assign the intercessory role to small groups or to special ministries. We can do so publicly and we can "walk the walk" in addition to "talking the talk." We may have some level of success as we do this. We may even raise up an entire congregation that looks not to the pastor for intercession but to the broader body of Christ as expressed in small-group fellowship.

How wonderful! We should celebrate when such things occur. Yet at the same time we live in a world in which many church members in many places still carry with them an unstated but deeply held expectation that the minister will be a person of prayer and that in a time of crisis, it is the prayers of the minister that will "count the most."

Of course this thinking is a fallacy. Do you suppose it is the only fallacy out there in the pews? Perhaps not.

Meanwhile, it is a common reality that a pastor is expected to be a man or woman of prayer. He or she is expected to fulfill an intercessory role on behalf of the needs of the flock. And at times he or she is held up also as an intermediary of sorts—a go-between who has special access to God and whose prayers are thus routed more directly to the server, straight through the firewall, right into God's own inbox. This should not be so, but meanwhile it is.

King

With the exception of a pastor we'll mention later in this book who was driven onto his new campus in the back of a shiny Corvette, most pastors are not given the royal treatment as they arrive. Every once in a while a congregation does something "over the top" for its minister, usually on a service anniversary such as twenty-five or thirty years. One pastor we know received a Mercedes for his thirty-year service anniversary, but before this chapter becomes all about the cars, let us simply say that most pastors will be driving their own

Hyundais—not tooling around in an exotic European sedan that the church graciously gifted to them.

When we speak of the pastor's role as king, we are not talking about royal robes, ornate thrones, or other trappings of high office. Instead we are talking about administration and oversight, two areas in which today's pastors may be the least prepared for duty.

"I'd be a better pastor if I went back to school and got an MBA," one suburban minister told us recently. His church has grown from a start-up just a few years ago to now over twelve hundred in weekend attendance. Although such growth was always the hope and aim of the church, the growth has brought issues—hiring and managing staff, building and maintaining a new campus, oversight of dozens of teams of volunteers—that the busy pastor does not feel equipped to handle.

"I was trained to study God's Word and to teach it with intelligence and passion," this pastor reports. "That's where my heart is, and that's where my gifts are. But honestly, most days around here I need an MBA! We are running a fairly substantial business around here, and I don't feel remotely qualified to lead or guide a business. I'm a preacher!"

The majority of working pastors may not be coping with the "problems" of growing from zero to twelve hundred in attendance. Yet if they are honest, many ministers will tell you that managing the business side of the church is one of their greatest challenges. Many of these pastors serve in places where there is not a full-time church secretary or receptionist. Many of these pastors do not have any other ministerial staff to help carry the load. And increasingly, many of today's pastors are bivocational, meaning that they are working at a secular job during the week and pulling together a meaningful worship experience on the weekend. Meanwhile they are pastors on a 24/7/365 basis, expected to be on call and available for emergencies, hospital visits, and more.

So when we speak of the kingly role of a pastor, we are talking about the dimension of leadership that is expressed through wise administration of resources, human and material. This kind of management training is usually not in the core curriculum of a Bible college or seminary. Along with basic people skill issues such as conflict resolution and managing difficult people, courses in business management could be a valuable addition to the training of today's—and tomorrow's—ministers.

The pastor as king is not expected to rule over his subjects or to wear crowns and robes while carrying out the duties of the office. Rather, the pastor as king is expected to faithfully manage and maintain many aspects of the business of church life. In some cases if the pastor does not manage these things, no one does.

These three roles—being a prophet, priest, and king—do not present us with a full-orbed picture of pastoral ministry and the expectations that come along with it. However, they do give us a good sense of some of the key expectations—exhortation, intercession, administration—that for most pastors will simply come with the job as they assume the leadership of a congregation.

When we better understand the expectations that burden those who serve us in ministry, we can better understand how to serve those who serve, and minister to those who minister.

Questions for Reflection

Pastors and Ministers

1. Mark ended up in a church where he was allowed to preach but was not allowed to actually lead the church in terms of direction or decision. He occupied the visible role of leader, a role he viewed as being a mere figurehead, while the actual leader was a wealthy layman. Might you have stayed in this place longer than Mark did? Would you have fled sooner for some reason, once you realized the true nature of the new setting? Would you have somehow tried to "fight" the established (and quite wealthy) leader of this congregation? Would you have left also, or would you still be there?

2. The gracious Southern gentleman who welcomed Mark and Janet turned out to have a massive and quite disproportionate influence over the church and its priorities. Have you personally witnessed examples or situations where a deep-pocketed donor either ruled the church or tried to rule it? If the donor is well-intentioned, nice to people, and consistently generous, how much influence should he or she have over matters of church priorities and decisions? A lot of influence? A little influence? No influence at all?

3. Although you may not normally use the word "prophet" when describing pastoral ministry, did you understand its use in this chapter? If you were ranking the role of exhortation among other pastoral duties and expectations, where would exhortation rank in the mix? How important is effective preaching and proclamation in the work of pastoring a local congregation? Where does this duty rank in relation to other issues of church life?

4. Although you may not normally use the word "priest" (it sounds so "high church," doesn't it?) when describing pastoral ministry, did

you understand its use in this chapter? If you were ranking the role of intercessory prayer among other pastoral duties and expectations, where would intercession rank in the mix? How important is prayer ministry in the work of pastoring a local congregation? Where does this duty rank in relation to other issues of church life? Should a local pastor's prayer life—or the lack of it—be a private issue, or is it the church's business to know how much, or if, its pastor is spending time on his or her knees in intercessory prayer?

5. Although you probably never use the word "king" when describing pastoral ministry, did you understand its use in this chapter? If you were ranking the role of administration among other pastoral duties and expectations, where would effective management of resources rank in the mix? How important is good business management in the work of pastoring a local congregation? Where does this duty rank in relation to other issues of church life? Is this the kind of duty that you believe a pastor should be trained to fulfill, or would you prefer that pastors left administration and management to others and just stuck to their preaching?

Local Churches and Church Boards

1. How often has your church been in transition, between pastors? During those times of transition, was your local church more interested in hiring a great speaker, a person with an extraordinary prayer life, or someone with a lot of business experience who could balance a budget and manage staff, leading an organization toward financial success?

2. Have you ever known a pastor who was simultaneously gifted in at least two of these areas—perhaps a great speaker with a deep inner spiritual life or perhaps a great businessperson who could also teach well? To what extent have you personally observed pastors with

more than one of the three roles (prophet, priest, king) as a personal strength? In your view, how rare is it for a prospective pastor to be exceptionally strong in more than one of these three major areas of pastoral responsibility?

3. Would your church intentionally hire a pastor who couldn't preach well, because he or she was a person of prayer or because he or she was smart in a business setting? Or—as is perhaps more likely—is strength in the pulpit more of a non-negotiable that must be present in your pastor, despite what other giftings may be present or absent?

4. Have you ever seen a pastor "succeed" in ministry despite a fairly poor pulpit performance? If so, what was the secret of that pastor's success? Did he or she simply show Christ's love to people to a great degree—a love that covered over the lack of giftedness in the pulpit? How does a pastor succeed in ministry, if he or she cannot teach or speak well? Is success possible for such pastors?

Denominational Leaders

1. When you are interviewing pastors to serve at churches within your territory, is there a role among these three (prophet, priest, and king) that you tend to value more highly or respect more fully than the others? Do you favor pastors who are strong orators, bringing excellence in the pulpit to their new setting? Do you personally gravitate to the more spiritually-minded ministers out there, whose prayer life causes you to reflect, listen, and learn? Do you look for pastors with keen business acumen and strong administrative skills? Generally speaking, which of the three roles seems more valuable to ministry? Which are you trying to find?

2. Have you met any or many persons who genuinely excel in all three of these major aspects of the pastoral role? Have you met any or many

persons who are simultaneously excellent preachers with abundant gifts for teaching, with rich lives as intercessors and experienced and wise managers who can lead a business toward strength and success? Is it possible—at least in theory—that such a person may exist? Have you ever met even one person who fits this description?

3. Larger churches often divide the roles, with the senior pastor handling the prophet tasks (preaching and teaching) while others cover the other bases. An executive pastor may handle the kingly role— hiring and reviewing staff, working on budget issues, coordinating a building process. An associate pastor may be tasked with the priestly roles such as leading prayer, small groups, or spiritual formation, freeing up the senior pastor to concentrate on teaching. Is there any way to deploy this method that is used by larger churches, so that small churches could also divide up the various pastoral roles? Could a layperson serve in administrative or spiritual ways, so as to free up the small-church pastor for duties in teaching and preaching? Why or why not?

4. How would you rate your own gifts in these three key areas? Are you better as prophet, better as priest, or better as king? Which of the three roles seems to best enable and equip you for your current venue of service? Do you believe that your gifting was a key factor in your selection for this current assignment in ministerial leadership and/or supervision? Why or why not?

FIVE

DYNASTY

WHEN ONE FAMILY CONTROLS THE CHURCH

"We studied all this stuff back in seminary," Terry relates with a wry grin. "And obviously I should have paid a lot more attention when we did!"

The busy and besieged pastor lets out a loud sigh before resuming his personal story. By Terry's choice we are meeting him at a location more than an hour's drive from his church, but he still glances over his shoulder occasionally, half expecting a parishioner to walk by.

Terry has been talking to us for twenty minutes now about a difficult situation he is facing in his current church—his second assignment in pastoral ministry. He is warming to his subject as he recalls his days of being a theology student, before taking his first pastorate.

"Dr. Martinson talked to us about this exact kind of situation going on in a church. He told us a tale about a church out in Kentucky somewhere that was controlled by one family. The in-laws and outlaws of this family managed the money, had a firm majority on the church board, and basically made all the major strategic decisions of the church.

"By then most of the players were dead, so our professor felt comfortable telling us about the actual situation and the real people that were involved.

"What I remember is that he walked us through the experiences of three consecutive pastors of this one particular church. Each pastor sooner or later got crosswise with the main family. Each pastor sooner or later got voted out or thrown out or just plain run out of town. And as far as we could tell, listening to the case study, all three pastors were basically normal, good-hearted guys who just wanted to get along. They weren't hardheaded or stubborn or difficult personalities, and let's face it—sometimes we pastors can be all of those things!"

Terry pauses again, thinking back to the classroom discussions.

"Dr. Martinson was gifted in telling stories. He had us laughing out loud as we worked on the case study of that congregation. Two of the three pastors had been in his classes over the years, so he had access to inside information about this specific congregation. He knew the inside details and the key players, and he used this case study with all of his practical theology students. He was hilarious and witty and we laughed so much as he described the case.

"But when the same thing happened to me in real life, it wasn't so funny."

Dynasty Myths and Legends

When we hear a tale of a single family controlling the life of a congregation, we often imagine a larger-than-life personality dominating the rest of the leaders. We may tend to picture a physically large male, outspoken and highly opinionated, who intimidates everyone around him, including his children. It's a phenomenon we'll discuss more fully in the next chapter, as we look at the dynamics of having a so-called church boss.

Within this chapter, however, we'll examine and unpack Terry's difficult situation because it illustrates a different type of dynasty and thus a separate type of dynamic within the church. We'll save the "church boss" discussion for the next chapter. Within this section we'll focus on a dynastic family with near-complete or total control of the decisions in a church. Before going further we'll stop and let Terry describe his initial interview with the church board, and his onset impressions as he agreed to serve this particular church. Not surprisingly, he didn't see the contours of his future issues. No one drew him a map of where the land mines had been laid in the church parking lot.

"I did a Skype interview before coming out here," Terry remembers. "The district superintendent wanted to save money. So instead of having the top two or three candidates travel to the church, the D.S. just set up Skype interviews with the handful of finalists. The church wanted the wives to be included in the interviews, so my wife and I sat in our own living room about seven hundred miles away from the church and stared into the webcam of our own computer. And of course, thanks to Skype, we could see a group of eight people, plus the D.S., sitting in one of the church meeting rooms.

"At that time there were only six people on the church board, but the superintendent had invited two other church members onto the search team. So altogether there were eight of them—nine if you count the district superintendent—and two of us. We did a Skype interview for almost ninety minutes that evening, and it went pretty well.

"What I noticed about the Skype session," Terry continues, "is how passive everyone seemed. There were eight people from the church—five women and three men. They were asking what I call 'softball' questions—easy things about my own gifts for ministry and my strategic priorities in ministry. Everyone was nice and polite and friendly, and the interview seemed to go well. And it must have gone well, because after that interview they did invite us to travel out to the church, preach for a Sunday morning service, and then meet with the church board in person. After that they ended up voting for me with a strong vote, so that was also a good sign.

"I could tell people were passive in general, and I also noticed that people were nice and polite and good-natured."

Terry stops his monologue for a moment as a young family wanders close to our table. Although we're not geographically close to the parish where he currently serves, he is cautious in talking to us about his challenges.

"Good-natured," he continues. "That was my onset impression. I had no idea what was behind some of those smiles! There was absolutely no sign of a typical church boss," Terry admits as he thinks back to the Skype interview and the later in-person meetings with the board members. "No one dominated the conversation, and I would add that there didn't seem to be a dominant personality in the whole group! In fact, when we finished the Skype time, my wife remarked about how genial and kindly everyone seemed.

"She was right about that," Terry continues. "People were friendly and agreeable and passive in general. They didn't ask us any difficult questions. They didn't show signs of a sarcastic or cynical attitude. Compared to my original church, I remember thinking that this group looked easy to manage, and easy to lead!

"As it turns out, I was completely wrong about that," he laments.

Romancing the Matriarch

When a congregation is dominated by a church boss, almost everyone can point to the specific person and describe his or her various controlling behaviors. Even if people are inclined not to disclose or discuss the true dynamics of their local church leadership, the personality and behaviors of a church boss tend to be visible and identifiable. The existence of a bossy personality cannot be hidden forever and is usually discernible even in initial impressions. The result is an overt situation that can be analyzed, prepared for, and perhaps successfully managed by the incoming pastor. If there is a presiding bishop or superintendent, this leader may be well aware of the identity and character of the so-called boss.

But what if the controlling family doesn't display a "church boss" type leader? And what if the dynasty within the local church is invisibly led by a small woman who leads with a quiet voice, guiding the outcomes from within her own family circle, rather than steering the church from a position of personal authority on the church board? In this type of case there is no overt church boss to confront, and the resulting passivity can provide effective camouflage that conceals the true dynamics of church decisions.

In Terry's case, the hidden leader of his church was a physically small grandmother, quiet and soft-spoken, who didn't have (or want) a seat on the board and who didn't tend to speak up in church meetings. Yet behind the scenes this quiet powerhouse was completely in control of the congregation's worship style, priorities, financial decisions, and more. As Terry began to discover after the conflict emerged, she had maintained this control for more than two decades of church life, while never officially serving in a visible role of leadership.

The unelected leader of Terry's congregation presided over a large family: four married daughters and their children. Three of the four married daughters were part of the congregation and two of those three husbands served on the church board. Among the five marriages—the matriarch and her husband, her four daughters and their four husbands—there was not an outspoken, dominant male personality anywhere in the mix. And although one daughter could be forthright and somewhat demanding, the other four women led from quietness rather than from visible demonstrations of verbal authority.

"After I'd been there for a while, I learned how things really were," Terry says very quietly. "I began telling my wife that our church was controlled by a cabal of women—that's the exact word I used. I'm sorry if that sounds harsh to you, and I guess I don't mean it theologically. But it really seemed that way as I learned more about how things really worked."

The unelected leaders of the church—all women, and none of them serving personally on the church board or in a visible role of leadership—took a fairly immediate dislike to Terry's wife. Although the initial interviews had gone well, the invisible leaders were quick to judge and condemn the wife of their new pastor, almost right from the start.

"My wife is a beautiful woman and an amazing person," Terry tells us with passion in his voice. (We wish she were sitting here with us to hear her husband describe her, but she is working at a hospital more than an hour's drive away from our lunch engagement.) "Another fact about my wife is that she tends to dress kind of casually, and some people might say she dresses like a man."

Terry stops his narrative entirely. He stares at us a moment.

"I don't want you thinking the wrong thing!" he exclaims. "My wife is very feminine and very much a woman. But she likes to dress in jeans and T-shirts or jeans and sweatshirts, and she is just a casual kind of person in how she dresses.

"As it turns out, the matriarch of the church and her cluster of daughters were all 'highly feminine' types. They had big hair, big jewelry, and flashy dresses—which are fairly normal in this part of the country—and they didn't like it at all when their new pastor's wife had short hair or straight hair or wore jeans all the time.

"Can you believe this stuff?" Terry asks us, shaking his head. "I mean, I am preaching my best sermons and I am leading as wisely as I can, and the church is gaining some new people, and without us knowing it, the entire leadership of the church has quietly turned against us because they don't like how my wife dresses or how she wears her hair.

"Did I miss this in seminary?" Terry now wonders aloud. "Did they tell us that the appearance of our wives might be the deciding factor in how effective our ministry would be in a local setting?"

Terry's voice trails off into silence.

"We didn't realize any of this at first," he says. "When we processed all of this later, we remembered that my wife had been wearing a skirt and blouse for our Skype interview—an entirely new outfit that she bought for job-hunting in our new location. So if the interviewers were looking at my wife during the Skype session, they would have seen her looking more 'typically' female than she usually looks in her real life. Trust me on this one—we didn't do that to create some sort of impression! She just wore that particular outfit because it was new, and we were both going to be staring into a webcam all evening, and she wanted to look nice.

"Knowing what we know now, my wife's choice of outfit for the Skype session may have helped me get the job," Terry laughs harshly. "But her fashion sense that night just wasn't how she looks all the time, or even how she usually looks. She is a beautiful person, and also, a woman who dresses casually and doesn't wear much makeup. I love her for that!"

We ask Terry to describe what was happening in the church (or not happening) before he figured out what the real issues were. Terry pauses for a moment and launches into a discussion of no-action church board meetings and always-delayed votes on minor issues.

"Carol's husband, Roger, has been on the church board for decades now," Terry admits, "but so far as I know he has never caused a problem or raised a fuss. He sits there in most of our meetings kind of quietly, not saying very much. Two of his sons-in-law are on the board and they have very similar personalities to his. They show up, they are always on time, they are reliable and dependable, and they don't say much. I can't remember any of them ever causing a problem or taking over a meeting. They are nice guys: I genuinely like them!

But none of them is the leader of their own households, and maybe that tells you everything you need to know, right there. I didn't pick up on that right away. I must be slow!"

Not until six or eight months into his tenure did Terry realize that one woman had so much influence over the opinions and perspectives of everyone else. What he did notice prior to that time is that the church board would usually not complete any vote the first time an issue was raised. Instead the issue would be delayed until a later meeting, no matter what the issue was. Even the simplest of issues, and the smallest of expenditures, was treated in the same way—instead of coming to a quick decision, the matter would be placed on the agenda for a later meeting.

"We literally couldn't adjust a service time slightly or re-paint the church sign out on the street or consider a different format for our Wednesday night gatherings or do anything else the first time it came up in a board meeting. Everyone would quietly listen to whatever I suggested or brought to the table, but we wouldn't take a vote. If I tried to force a vote, they would tell me that they needed more time to think it over. Some of them would say they needed time to pray about it before voting. They would make it a spiritual matter— we should all go home and pray about it.

"Maybe that should have been a clue!" Terry says, shaking his head. "I guess I should have been worried about that. I actually saw it as a good sign—these people were cautious and wise, and they wanted to make careful decisions. So when they wouldn't come to a conclusion in a meeting, I saw that as mostly positive.

"What I didn't realize is that they delayed a decision so that everything could be related, verbatim, to the women who actually control this church. The main woman's husband would come home and talk to her about everything. Meanwhile her daughter's husbands would come home and talk to them also. Once the women had gotten all the input from the men, they would light up the phone lines and start deciding what we should do. Eventually, once the women had talked among themselves, Carol would guide a discussion and the women would have their own informal vote on the matter. Then at our next board meeting, the husbands would show up, all friendly and nice, and vote whatever the women had decided.

"You know those bracelets that say WWJD?" Terry asks us rhetorically. "What would Jesus do? Well in my congregation those bracelets ought to say something like WWWD: What would the women do? And nobody would make a decision or take a vote or do anything else until after they checked out the women's opinions on the matter. There was no one who would go up against Carol and her daughters. There was no one who wanted to take on the church dynasty."

Terry sighs; his shoulders relax a bit.

"Honestly, I wouldn't be in so much trouble right now if I'd realized this a lot sooner," he admits. "If I'd known how things were, I could have been a lot nicer to Carol. I could have paid more attention to her, maybe flattered her a little bit. As it is, I ended up getting crosswise with her right from the start, and all because my wife likes the natural look and wears jeans all the time."

Terry grins again and makes eye contact with us.

"Once I figured this out, I called my predecessor," he tells us with a sheepish look on his face. "I wanted to find out how much he knew, and how his experience had gone. So I called him up, and I kind of played dumb on the phone, and I just asked him if he considered his experience here to be mostly positive."

Terry stops and waits for us to pay full attention.

"About a minute into our conversation he interrupted me," Terry laughs. "And he just said, 'How is Carol doing?' kind of quietly. Then he added, 'How are her daughters doing?' and then both of us didn't say anything. And then after that, all of a sudden, both of us started laughing and couldn't stop.

"I needed that laughter," Terry admits, "because I was the one who was still stuck with the problem. He was the guy who had escaped from all that and was now many miles away serving on another district.

"When he asked about Carol and her daughters, that told me everything I needed to know," Terry relates. "If you're talking about this congregation and this group of people, that just kind of says it all."

What about Bob? Our Dynasty Reigns

In smaller churches—congregations of one hundred members or less—the balance of power can be fairly easy to obtain and manage. One key family or extended family, especially if there are several generations represented, can gain a disproportionate control over the church directions, decisions, and outcomes.

Lay members of the church may be swifter to realize this than the pastor. Church board members talk together in the parking lot, they have lunch together during the week, and they interact as people and as friends. There is a type of bond between lay members of the church board that somewhat excludes the pastor—who is, after all, a paid professional, and who is also an employee of the board.

Among the laity, issues of power and dominance tend to be visible in a fairly short time. However, just because the dynamics are realized and understood does not mean that they will be verbally discussed or explained to the pastor.

"I couldn't get anyone to serve on my leadership board," Bob tells us in another coffee shop many miles away from where we met with Terry. "I had quality people in my congregation, businesspeople and key leaders, men and women. After getting to know them, I would invite them to be considered for the leader board and they would quietly tell me 'no thanks.'

"This happened time after time, person after person, until finally I began to doubt my own charisma or influence. Why were so many people saying 'no' to me when I invited them into the leadership circle? Why were they resisting my polite and sincere invitations? For me, I entered a season of self-doubt."

Bob pauses and then explains the hidden reality.

"Finally, after four or five amazing leaders had declined to be considered for the board, I asked one of them why he wouldn't serve. It was maybe not a polite question on my part, but I was really getting frustrated by then. If there was a problem with my leadership or my personality, I needed to know.

"I was totally surprised when the man answered my question so quickly," Bob continues. "He looked at me and he said, 'Pastor, everyone knows that the church board is controlled by the McLarens. And in case you haven't noticed, I am not a McLaren and my wife is not a McLaren. So, frankly, no matter what I think or my wife thinks, we aren't ever going to have a voice at the leadership level.'

"When he said that to me, very matter-of-factly and without sarcasm, I just stood there in shock," Bob confesses. "It was the first time anyone had told me about a church dynasty that was literally right there under my nose. By that time I'd been pastoring the church for almost two years and it was going great—numbers were up, giving was on the rise, and the district superintendent seemed to like me!

"We were doing great," Bob sighs, "but when I tried to add seasoned, mature leaders onto the board, no one would serve. I'm glad I finally asked someone what was going on. I'm also glad that he decided to tell me!"

Bob served another two years at that congregation, and left it on a comparatively high note. We can't resist asking him a few further questions.

"I can tell you my secret," Bob smiles. "Once I found out how things were, I just never crossed the McLarens. I played golf with one of them, I had frequent lunches with another one, and I kept my finger in the wind so I knew which way it was blowing. I never once got into trouble with them. In fact, to this day they like me and they talk about my tenure as pastor as being a highlight of the church!"

Bob realizes how his confession may sound to an outsider.

"Don't get me wrong," he tells us. "I didn't adjust my theology or walk away from my holiness heritage or anything like that. I just stayed out of trouble. I didn't take a controversial position on things, and I didn't go against a McLaren opinion. But once I realized what was happening behind the scenes, I started working on getting a new assignment. It took me about nine months to get a good option on the table, but it helped that my current church was going so well.

"And, honestly, my current church was going so well because I was deciding to get along with the McLarens, no matter what."

We ask Bob how things are going in his present assignment.

"Not perfectly, but pretty well," is how Bob sums up his situation. "I'm free to speak my mind, I'm free to share my true opinions, and in general people will follow me if I take the time to explain things carefully, and if I wait for the slower ones to catch up. I think as a younger pastor I was in too much of a hurry with things. Often I expected people to just follow me because I was right—not because they had done their own prayerful consideration of the issues. These days I am slower to spell things out and allow for more discussion and by the time we take a vote on something, we are usually in agreement as a group of leaders."

Bob's perspective seems wise and we tell him so.

"Yeah," he says with a slow grin, "I knew a lot when I started. What I didn't know was how to lead people and how to influence people. What I didn't know is that some churches are controlled, behind the scenes, by one major family or by one key group of people.

"When I look back now at my early pastoring, I'm kind of embarrassed," Bob tells us. "I had a very high opinion of myself, and I was impatient with others, usually the lay leaders or my regular volunteers. They didn't agree with me fast enough. They didn't get on board with my ideas quick enough to suit me. To me, that meant they were un-spiritual or not praying enough about things or whatever.

"As I look back, I tend to think now that I was the one who was unspiritual," Bob tells us quietly. "I'd like to think that these days I am more prayerful, more respectful of others, and more inclusive of diverse viewpoints. But even after saying that, let me tell you I'm glad I don't pastor the McLarens in this season of my life. I have lost my patience with people who play power games in the church. I'm not going to lay down my life for a group of people who are carnal or mean-spirited. I'm not going to subject my family to the whims of church tyrants.

"I'm serving a healthy group of people," Bob shares. "And I'm a little older and maybe a little wiser myself. So overall, this is the best season of my pastoral life and my personal ministry. I like the McLarens—from a distance. But I'm ready to lead healthy people in the direction of Christ and his ministry."

Signs You May Have a Dynasty in Place

1. Key decisions are deferred for a later vote on a regular basis. Instead of a lively debate followed by on-the-record voting, there is a motion to table things until later and later, and when the leadership board con-venes, the matter seems to be already decided.

2. Capable and qualified leaders decline to join an existing church board. One or two such examples may not indicate a trend, but if there is a con-sistent pattern of leaders declining to serve, look for a reason. Capable leaders may recognize and resist the imbalance of power.

3. Families at or near the core of the church cycle out to other churches, leaving the congregation after only a few years. If this trend exists within the service duration of more than one pastor, the issue may be lay-driven and based around the concentric power of a dynasty.

4. The congregation seems to be invisibly but tangibly divided between "outsiders" and "insiders," and the insiders are related by blood, marriage, or by a very close personal friendship.

Questions for Reflection

Pastors and Ministers

1. If you are a female serving as a pastor, how much has "dress code" been a factor in your ability to lead and influence the congregation? Are you expected to dress in a certain way in order to lead?

2. If you are a married male serving as a pastor, has your wife ever been judged on the basis of something superficial such as her hairstyle, her manner of dress, or her accent when she speaks? To what extent, if any, did this judgment limit or impact your ability to lead the congregation?

3. If Terry were a personal friend, would you counsel him to stay in this place of service or to seek another congregation? What would guide your advice and counsel to Terry?

4. If you were serving this congregation, would you see it as your personal mission to break the stranglehold of the dynastic family, or would you be more inclined to try to go along and get along with the key leaders?

5. When Bob realized that the McLarens were functionally in charge of his church, he chose to not oppose them. This led to an apparently "successful" season of ministry, though Bob quietly sought another place to serve. By visible and quantifiable standards, the church appears to have done well during Bob's tenure. Meanwhile, Bob found a healthier place to serve—a church with no dynasty. Did Bob make an honorable choice in deciding not to oppose the McLarens? Why or why not? Did Bob make a wise and ethical choice in deciding to look for another place to serve? Why or why not?

6. If you were serving as the senior or lead pastor, would you knowingly hire a member of the dynasty to be your associate pastor, worship leader, youth pastor, or similar role? Do you believe that acknowledging the power structures in a church by "including" them on the ministry staff is a wise strategy?

Local Churches and Church Boards

1. If your own church and congregation were basically under the control of a key family, would you explain this to a new pastor before he or she said yes to the congregation's call? Why or why not?

2. How does your church help a pastor's wife feel welcomed and included in the life of the congregation? When the pastor is male, who reaches out to be a friend to his wife as the family tries to fit in to the new setting? Who in your congregation tries to "give" to the pastoral family, instead of waiting to "receive" from the parsonage team?

3. If you discovered that your own congregation were ruled by an unseen dynasty (an extended family group or network) would you personally be more likely to leave the church, stay and fight, or stay and get along? Which choice more typically reflects your own behavior and preference?

Denominational Leaders

1. Is it your policy to conduct exit interviews with pastors as they leave a particular place of service? If so, does your process of discovery include any specific questions about the use or misuse of financial and political power within the congregation?

2. If a pastor on your own district left a church in response to a dynasty problem, do you believe that you would be aware of the true

dynamics of the situation? If you were aware, how much of this information would you share with prospective pastoral candidates? Would you, in any sense, warn them about the political realities they might be about to encounter?

3. If Terry were serving under your leadership, would you be encouraging him to remain in this place of service, despite his lack of traction, or would you be ready to help him find a new assignment? What do you believe is best for Terry and his wife and for the local congregation?

4. Do you have any personal experience with breaking a dynasty, either as a pastor or as a presiding denominational official? Have you successfully dislodged a controlling family so that a church could find its way to health, moving forward to effective ministry?

5. In your opinion, what is the best strategy for an incoming pastor who is about to serve a dynastic church? Should he or she simply get along with the controlling group for as long as possible? Would you encourage your pastor to curry favor with the controlling group, in order to keep the peace and avoid the outbreak of destructive conflict? Why or why not?

SIX

DUKES

OF

HAZARD

DEALING WITH A CHURCH BOSS

"We met him on our third day of serving at Rosemount," Gary tells us as he begins a narration about his encounter with a church boss. Nearly forty but looking a decade or so younger, Gary has a boyish grin and a youthful presence that belies his nearly two decades in pastoral ministry. After serving as a student ministries pastor in two larger-sized churches, Gary prayed and accepted his first call to be a teaching pastor. It is his experience in that role—his first time to serve as the senior pastor—that led us to contact Gary and schedule an interview with him.

Three different ministers have told us that if we want to hear a great story about a church boss, we should go meet Gary. By the time we've heard this twice, we tend to believe our volunteer informants. When the third recommendation rolls in, we send Gary an e-mail note and arrange to meet him at a thriving Panera Bread store across town from the place where he currently serves.

With pens and our trusted mini-recorder at the ready, it's time to start our planned interview with this successful minister.

Gary, who doesn't appear pretentious at all, nods his head as we begin.

"Listen, I'm just gonna give this to ya straight," he says with a faint trace of a Southern dialect. "I could embellish this thing and draw it all out for a long time, but I'm just going to describe what happened as simply and quickly as I can. If you two want to dress it up for your book, go right ahead. But I'm telling you, the story itself doesn't need much help!"

We ask Gary to tell us more about his first encounter with a difficult and demanding church boss.

"It's day three for us in this place; we have literally just arrived to serve here. We're in a small parsonage that's about a mile or so from the church property. Right now it's maybe eight o'clock in the morning," Gary continues. "My wife is still in her bathrobe, and I am only wearing a T-shirt and my favorite pair of boxers. I'm reading the newspaper on the couch in the living room. My wife is trying to make coffee in the kitchen. There is a stack of boxes next to me by the couch and a long trail of boxes leading down the main hall."

Gary pauses a moment, looking at us carefully.

"Listen, since you're quoting me in your book I should probably claim that I've been up since 5 a.m. poring over the Old Testament in the original Hebrew. I should probably make up a story that I have just finished my two-hour morning prayer time, right? But it's only our third day in this place and we aren't sleeping well yet. We're hearing strange noises at night and we haven't found the box with the good sheets in it and we're barely functional. We are still in the process of getting moved in here. It's 8 a.m. and my wife and I are just starting our day together, okay?"

Gary smiles and continues.

"It's only our third day in my first assignment as a senior pastor. As I've said, we aren't even fully unpacked yet. We just unloaded the moving truck on a Monday afternoon and I'm due to preach on the following Sunday. Right now it's Wednesday morning and we have boxes all over the place. I'm in my underwear—my wife's in her bathrobe. Are you two getting the picture here? Do you hear me? It's day three!"

Gary shakes his head, remembering the moment.

"Anyway, I'm sitting there in the living room and I hear this knock at the door, kind of a loud bang. It takes me a split second to realize—hey, it's eight in the morning and someone just knocked on my front door.

"We hear this knock, and then, *wham*! The door opens and a guy walks right into our front entry hall. He's got a cup of coffee in one hand and a big metal toolbox in the other hand. He knocks just one time, and the next thing we know—he's walking right into our house like he lives there!"

Gary lets out a huge sigh.

"That's exactly the way we met Art," Gary relates. "And if that one moment doesn't give you the whole picture, then maybe you're not paying attention!"

All three of us laugh.

Gary goes on to describe how a church boss, carrying his own set of keys to the parsonage, has come over to make some much-needed repairs. He is doing this without even checking with the new pastor to establish a convenient time or to set up a confirmed appointment. Instead, consulting only his own personal schedule and his own personal preferences, this unelected church boss has decided to do the repairs at whatever time suits him best.

Gary fills in a few other details while we wait patiently, hoping to ask him the question that's foremost in our minds. Finally, during a pause in the narration, we ask Gary what we want to know.

"How did you deal with the problem that morning?"

Gary makes a wry face and sips his coffee.

"I didn't know what to do," he sighs. "I stood up, rushed into the entry hall, stared into the face of this guy, and honestly I didn't even know where to start with him! I wanted to yell at him for barging into my house uninvited, but something stopped me from being that assertive. Plus I'm in my boxers, right? So I don't feel very authoritative or forceful or particularly impressive in that moment."

Gary's voice trails off into silence.

Then he smiles, remembering the moment.

"My wife ducks into the pantry," he grins. "We have this small walk-in pantry in the kitchen area and my wife literally ducks in there and half-closes the door. She is expecting me to deal with the guy. She's the one who's at least got a robe on and I'm standing there in just my boxers and a T-shirt. Between the two of us, she is a lot more presentable than I am, but she's not about to confront this guy. She is hiding out in our new pantry, praying to Jesus!"

Gary laughs out loud.

The rookie pastor goes on to describe his first conversation with the uninvited intruder. Without apparent shame or discomfort, the gentleman who has walked in unannounced ends up being more aggressive and assertive. It's the unwelcome guest who has the upper hand during the conversation, at least at the start.

"This is the only time I can possibly do this," Gary remembers Art telling him about the needed repairs. As of that Wednesday morning Gary didn't know Art personally and didn't yet realize that Art was retired. The new pastor didn't know that his sudden intruder was without a formal schedule at all and could literally be available almost any time of the day or night. Meanwhile, church boss Art is telling his new pastor that right now—8 a.m. on day three—is the only possible time that certain parsonage repairs can be completed. And the pastor doesn't know any better, for the moment.

Gary sighs again, and returns to his story.

"Anyway, I breathed a quick prayer and then asked Art to please come back in about twenty minutes or so," Gary recalls. "I kind of pushed him back out the front door without waiting for his answer. Then I grabbed my wife out of the pantry where she was hiding. Both of us ran back to the bedroom and put some clothes on, and then I took her to McDonald's for breakfast while we figured out what to do next.

"The whole time all this is happening—during the twenty-minute delay that I had asked for—Art is sitting out in my driveway in his truck, not going anywhere. Apparently he is just going to sit out there until the twenty minutes are up, then he's planning to walk right back into my house and do whatever he came over to do.

"So once we get our clothes on, my wife and I walk out the door of our own house, maybe ten minutes after Art has walked in, and there he is, sitting in his truck, blocking our driveway. So I walk up to the window on the driver's side, knock on the window, and ask Art to move out of the way so we can get our car out and leave for a while. My wife and I get into our car, back out of the driveway, and drive to Mc-Donald's. My wife is shaking—literally shaking—because she is so upset by all of this. And while we drive to McDonald's both of us are thinking, 'Wow, maybe we shouldn't have said yes to this church!'"

Signs of the Times

While the new pastor and his wife are eating an impromptu breakfast nearby, the church boss goes ahead and begins the planned repairs, making a major mess at the parsonage. About an hour later, when Gary and his wife return to their house, there is no sign of Art or Art's truck, but there are tools laying everywhere in the kitchen and a few more tools in the front entry hall. And there is a note taped to the kitchen sink saying "Do not use until fixed."

There is no way to know when, if, or how Art plans to come back and fix the kitchen sink. The frazzled young pastor, having never met Art before this morning's encounter, hasn't yet acquired Art's cell phone number. So a parsonage that is already strewn with moving boxes and half-unpacked luggage now has the added dimension of tools and repairs and half-finished projects here and there. Is it safe to keep unpacking and getting settled? Should they wait and see what the repair situation is, before getting fully moved in?

Gary shakes his head and looks down at the ground.

"I can't believe we put up with all that," he says quietly. "We got back home after having our breakfast, and our new house was still being invaded. I mean, Art was gone at that time, but his tools and his sticky notes were all over our house. And we had no idea when he would walk in the door next. Was he coming back right now? Would he walk in an hour from now? Would we see him the next morning at the same time, all over again? We had no way of knowing."

In a busy Panera with a lot of ambient noise, all three of us are silent.

Finally Gary finds his voice.

"I remember thinking when I drove to McDonald's that I had won the first round," Gary admits. "I remember thinking that by backing him out the door, and making him wait twenty minutes, maybe I was gaining the upper hand.

"Wow, was I wrong about that. When we got back home, and found our new home strewn with tools and signs and projects everywhere, and there was no clue about Art's plans, and no way to get ahold of him, that's when I knew that I wasn't winning. Right then and there I wanted to go back to seminary, back to all of my major professors, and just kind of say, 'What am I supposed to do *now*?'"

Gary meets our gaze with a wry smile.

"That morning I didn't realize I was dealing with a church boss—at least, not yet," Gary confides. "All I knew was that I had a rogue church repairman with his own set of keys and his own agenda. Silly me—I thought that problem was fixable once I sat down with the church board."

Gary's next meeting with the church board, which would also be his first meeting with the board since becoming the senior pastor, wasn't scheduled to take place for another two weeks. Meanwhile, the parsonage was in evident and sorrowful disarray. And the first lady of the parsonage, surprised in her bathrobe on her third day in her new home, was ready to re-pack the moving truck, back it out of the driveway, and flee to another town.

"That's maybe a bit melodramatic," Gary admits as he tells us about his wife's perspective. "But she has a strong sense of privacy, and she felt like her privacy had totally been invaded. It was like someone had broken into our home and stolen from us. She didn't feel safe anymore!"

Gary, being sensitive to his wife's point of view, decided to take the matter to the church board immediately. Why wait? The sooner this problem got solved, the better things would be. So Gary grabbed a phone list, dialed the chairman of the church board, and started to explain the dilemma.

"He cut me off before I even got started," Gary remembers. "Here I am trying to find some sympathy with the leader of the church board, and he won't even listen to my point of view. He starts telling me 'Well, that's just Art' and 'Isn't it wonderful that Art is willing to fix all these things?' and I'm thinking, this guy doesn't get it!"

Hanging up the phone after the call, Gary was more frustrated than ever. His wife was even more so. The two of them decided to ask for an emergency meeting of the church board right away. It was Wednesday, and by working the phones aggressively, Gary was able to get the board to assemble on Saturday morning.

From among eight men and three women serving on the leadership board, Gary had seven men and one woman at the emergency meeting. Gary attempted to explain his situation carefully and without attacking Art's reputation. He framed the meeting as a request for advice and counsel—how should he and his wife proceed, given this situation?

"There was quick consensus on the matter," Gary remembers. "The leader of the board reminded everyone that Art was working for free—the church wasn't paying him to do the repairs. So apparently, if you're willing to work for free, you can barge in on the pastor and his wife anytime—no appointment needed!"

There was more to the story. Art had generously offered to buy some needed parts without being reimbursed by the church. The church, which was already paying a moving allowance to relocate their new pastor, had been very receptive to Art's generous offer to simply buy the replacement parts.

"How can we turn that away?" Gary remembers one board member asking. "If the guy is willing to work for free and he's also willing to buy the parts and not get paid back by the church, we should be lining up to shake his hand and say thank you! The worst thing we could possibly do is complain about his timing!"

Gary, in his first assignment as a lead pastor, was dumbfounded. He had expected support, agreement, and encouragement from these leaders. Instead he discovered that the leadership group supported Art—and wanted Gary and his wife to be grateful and thankful that their privacy had been invaded!

If there was a way forward, Gary couldn't see it clearly.

A half-dozen Art stories later, we ask Gary what he did after that initial emergency session with the leadership board.

"Well, I didn't know what to do," Gary admits. "So I talked it over with my wife, and we decided to change the locks immediately. I literally drove home from the board meeting that Saturday, talked things over with my wife, and then we went to Home Depot and bought all new locks. I came home, took off all the door locks, and replaced them with new locks and new keys."

Problem solved.

Or more accurately—problem escalated.

"Sure enough, Art came back on the following Tuesday. He hadn't called first or asked permission or set up an appointment with us. About a week after his first surprise visit he just showed up for his second surprise visit. No notice. No call.

"I was gone at the time. In fact, I was at the hospital meeting with a sick elder and his wife. My wife was home, and when she heard Art rattling the lock she was tempted to call the police! Instead she hid out in the house, half expecting Art to be a professional locksmith, and didn't really exhale until Art quit trying to break in to our house.

"She called me while that was happening," Gary smiles. "She was whispering in the phone that Art was there. She was half worried about it and half amused that Art couldn't get past the new locks."

Behind the scenes, Art swung into motion with much more political clout than the new pastor had yet amassed. Although Art was not a current board member, he had long been the loudest and most important voice in the church's major decisions. Phone call by phone call, Art canvassed the board members. He arranged for the group to gather without inviting Gary or his wife to the meeting. At this unscheduled and quite out-of-order meeting of the church board, Art spoke passionately about the problem and what needed to be done.

Not surprisingly, Art succeeded in his quest.

Meeting behind the pastor's back, the board passed a policy saying that if the pastor changed the locks at the parsonage, every board member had to be given the new key within two days of the change. In addition, anyone on the designated church work crew—a group that conspicuously included Art—also had to be issued a new key to the parsonage.

Vote taken, motion passed, matter settled.

The pastor was informed by written memo, which was laid on the desk in his church office, to which the board members also had keys.

"I called them on it," Gary fumes. "I was hot. I mean, I tend to have kind of a fiery temper anyway, but this time I was really hot. When I found out about the new policy I called the chairman of the board and I really chewed him out. I told him that instead of being supportive of his pastor, he was being supportive of the problem. I told him that he needed to look at this whole thing a lot differently. I told him I was personally disappointed in him, and I was disappointed in his leadership."

Gary stops talking and stares off into the distance.

"That was a stupid thing to do, I admit that," Gary sighs. "But I was hot. What was the point of getting new locks if I had to run around and give everyone in the whole church a set of keys to my house? Okay, obviously I'm exaggerating a little bit, but what's the point of new keys, if you give them to everyone?"

Before the new pastor had even had a chance to lead and guide the congregation, battle lines were formed and open conflict had emerged. On one side, Gary and his wife felt abandoned and unloved, believing that no one had their best interests in mind. Yet from the board's perspective, the parsonage belonged to the church. The structure was the property of the church, not the pastor. So it was entirely appropriate that the church board members and work crew members have keys to the structure that the church owned.

"I look back at that situation, and I wish I had handled it differently," Gary says with a quiet certainty.

He pauses long enough to make sure we're listening.

"I often wish I would have just re-packed our big truck and moved out—like my wife suggested," he admits wistfully. "After the way things got started there, my ministry at Rosemount never really got off the ground. It was doomed from the beginning, I guess."

Gary's pastoral service to that congregation lasted for fifteen months. Much of the time was spent in conflict about choices, decisions, and directions for the future of the church. It seemed to Gary that no matter what he proposed, Art and the board had a differing opinion. Having angered Art right from the start, the new pastor believed that he was doomed to opposition from the leaders. Whether or not this was a self-fulfilling prophecy, it is exactly the way things worked out.

A little more than a year after unpacking into the parsonage, Gary resigned, moved three states away, and accepted a recruiting job at a well-known Christian university. He left pastoral ministry behind and says he has no plans to return to serving a local congregation any time soon.

"There were probably a half-dozen major decisions that I tried to lead during my time at Rosemount," Gary says. "And in each one of those decisions the church board backed Art and his perspective, rather than following my leadership. Maybe some of my trouble was of my own making, I can see that. But you have to admit it's very strange when a church board would rather follow an unelected layman than follow their duly elected and God-called spiritual leader!"

Now separated from the experience by more than six years, Gary's emotions are still near the surface. He enjoys working for the college, recruiting students from several nearby states, but when he talks about pastoral ministry, you can hear the raw emotions in the voice of this talented ex-pastor.

Dominance and Submission

Gary's encounter with a church boss may be highly specific—a guy walks into a parsonage—but the general situation is familiar. Over time, one individual exercises an unusual amount of influence over the leadership of a church, with the result that any given pastor may be considered subordinate to, or in a lesser role than, the person who holds the political influence.

Across multiple variables such as denomination, location, church size, and other demographic issues, certain similarities emerge when studying the typology of a church boss. The church boss is most often male, generally middle-aged to older, and may have been a part of the congregation for decades. Over time, the passive nature of many lay leaders and board members may have caused them to accept and adjust to the behavior and character of the boss. When this happens, the result is that church leaders tend to make excuses for the boss's bad conduct rather than confronting it, or insisting on healthy procedures and structure.

"Oh, that's just Art," Gary remembers being told by one leader.

Or as another board member put it: "Well, Art has always been the main guy around here, and let's face it—he unloads a lot of his money in the offering plate!" Whether tacitly or explicitly expressed, the (faulty) general precept is that if someone contributes a lot of money or offers a lot of help, they have a right to dominate, control, and lead the congregation. This pattern is repeated time after time and is most visible in smaller churches with a correspondingly smaller financial base.

Whether or not the church boss is a major financial contributor and whether or not the controlling personality offers genuine and useful service to the church, domineering or unspiritual conduct can be toxic in a congregation. Bad conduct left unchecked is lethal to overall spiritual health.

Pastors may shuffle through in short-term assignments, never staying long enough to see their ministry bear fruit. Visitors may quickly tire of the visible, divisive church politics. Meanwhile the congregation languishes in a slow or no-growth environment, failing to meaningfully impact its community for Christ. Over time the leadership emphasis may shift to mundane priorities such as painting the building, buying new carpet, or installing a new sign. While neutral in themselves, such priorities may indicate the lack of spiritual leadership and/or the presence of a church boss within the congregation.

Presiding denominational leaders, whether or not aware of the church boss, may be reluctant to interfere in the inner workings of a local congregation. One pastor recalls going to his immediate superior with a church boss problem, only to be told, "Try to get along with him. Things will go a lot better for you if you do!"

While this advice may be wise and may have been the result of significant prayer or spiritual reflection, the pastor went away sorrowful. He had hoped that perhaps a higher-echelon leader would ride to his rescue and confront the difficult dynamics posed by the church boss. Such hopes were quickly dashed by the denominational leader's lack of interest in getting involved.

Behaviors that Typify a Church Boss

1. The spiritual leadership and valid authority of the pastor is not held in high regard. Instead, there is a focus on congregational longevity (e.g., how long someone has been around) or the impact of financial participation (e.g., contributions in the offering plate). The idea of the pastor being someone with personal spiritual wisdom and elected positional authority is simply not valued or realized. Instead, authority is derived from political power.

2. Policies and procedures put in place by the church board are ignored if they do not prove to be convenient. Or perhaps the church boss may prevail in getting policies and procedures changed, with or without pastoral approval and participation in the process. Either way, official church board policy is regarded as a trivial and changeable matter.

3. The church boss operates with a high degree of personal autonomy, and a low interest in layers of authority, good process, or written records.

One typical church boss, not a current member of the church board, had led the counting of church offerings for more than a decade. He simply refused to give up the role, and the board was not strong enough to overcome his objections. Two separate pastors cycled through the church and were also unable to "liberate" the counting of the weekly offerings. Not surprisingly there was a lack of transparency in the counting process, and frequently the offerings were counted off-site, in the home of the church boss. Even if there is no actual intent to defraud, this kind of process creates the appearance of real or potential misconduct.

4. Even when confronted about his or her behavior or conduct, the church boss may ignore the wishes, requests, or written instructions from a pastor or the elected church board. Such behavior points to the need for an effective church discipline within local congregations, following clear procedures and with due process for all. The absence of church discipline in a local congregation creates exactly the kind of environment in which a church boss may rise to prominence and political power, then cling to it over a long period of time.

Questions for Reflection

Pastors and Ministers

1. If you had a church boss who insisted on counting the offering and often counted the money off-site, perhaps days after the services, would you allow that kind of situation to continue? If not, what action steps would you take to bring about transparent, contemporaneous, and multiply-witnessed counting of church funds? In the real world, how would you remove control of this issue from a church boss and establish effective control by the elected board and/or a properly configured counting or offerings committee?

2. As we recall Gary's story, he asked for and received an emergency meeting of the church board but was shocked when the board supported the church boss (intruder) rather than the pastor and his wife (residents of the parsonage). Were you shocked by this reaction by the board? Why or why not?

3. If you moved to a new assignment and discovered a church boss in place, would you share this information with your presiding district superintendent? Why or why not? If you did share the information, would you expect a specific response or intervention on the part of the district leader?

4. In your view, to what extent should a church board have the pastor's back in matters pertaining to peace, quiet, and family life? In your view, to what extent should a district leader have the pastor's back in these same kinds of matters? In your view, should every pastor bear the burden of protecting himself or herself, or should someone, somewhere, be protecting the pastor and his or her family?

5. If you or a member of your family were victimized in some way by a church boss, would you tell someone? Would you talk about it? Who would you trust to understand and support your own perspective?

Local Churches and Church Boards

1. Have you ever been a part of a congregation or a church board that was ruled by an unelected leader? If so, did this seem like a healthy situation to you? Do you believe that having such a church boss was in the best interest of your board, your congregation, and your pastor?

2. When Pastor Gary and his wife went out and got new keys made for the locks on the parsonage, can you understand why they did this? If you had been serving on the board and the parsonage thus "belonged" to you, would you have been upset or offended that the pastor changed the locks?

3. One of Pastor Gary's feelings was that if he didn't defend himself, no one else was going to defend him. In your view, who (if anyone) should defend a pastor and protect his or her privacy, peacefulness, and family life? Is the pastor supposed to protect himself or herself, or do you believe that one function of a church board is to come alongside its pastor with support, encouragement, and (if necessary) protection?

4. If you were serving on a church board that was being dominated by one person or by a church boss, would you welcome or want the intervention or participation of a denominational leader, such as a district superintendent? Why or why not? Have you ever seen a denominational leader try to help a local congregation with this type of problem or issue? If so, was the situation resolved in a way that produced a healthy structure of governance?

Denominational Leaders

1. If a pastor under your direct supervision came to you with the type of a problem described by Gary in this chapter, would you advise the minister to stay and fight or to relocate to a new assignment? Which is the wiser and better course of action for the pastor as a minister of the gospel?

2. Do you believe that most local churches are better off being left alone with their church boss? That is, that "don't rock the boat" is the best policy for dealing with these situations? Conversely, do you believe that the long-term health of the congregation might be best served by some type of intervention in order to restore or install democracy, transparency, and/or healthy leadership practices?

3. Have you ever seen or used, developed or implemented a specific policy for dealing with a congregation or pastor that is being dominated by a church boss? In your view, does such a method or curriculum currently exist? Does your own denomination have a resource of this type?

SEVEN

GUNSMOKE

ARE SHOOT-OUTS IN
THE CORRAL REALLY OK?

Richard is an active-duty chaplain serving in the United States Armed Forces. In his first four years of military service he has already received two specific honors for his conduct and behavior. Both citations mentioned his bravery under duress; both also mentioned his caring and compassion for others. He has already risen in rank and seems poised to keep rising in the well-regulated military environment.

He has graciously agreed to connect with us.

We'll be talking with Richard not because of what he is now: a decorated and honored military chaplain. Instead, our interest in Richard is formed by his previous experience as an active-duty pastor in two evangelical congregations. By his choice and ours we are not mentioning the specific denomination in which he served.

The chaplain arrives in uniform, right on time.

"It is good to finally meet you two in person!" Richard smiles as he joins us.

After a few moments of pleasant conversation, we ask Richard the self-evident questions: "Are you enjoying your service? Does the military seem like a good fit for your gifts and graces? Are you glad you made this change in your ministerial career?"

The slender, ultra-fit chaplain smiles his response.

"I know what you're doing here," he grins, "and I enjoyed reading over the sample questions you sent me. I'm glad to help with your project. I spent my early years in pastoral ministry, serving two different churches. As you know, I decided to make a transition into chaplaincy and military service. It wasn't an easy choice to make, but, yes, I am glad I made the decision. I'm also glad to talk about why I changed the focus of my ministry and how these two different kinds of ministry—pastoring and being a chaplain—are actually quite similar."

Richard shifts his weight in his chair and looks across the table directly. His demeanor is serious, but there is still a light of humor in his eyes.

"After being a pastor for a while," says the young officer, "I decided that if I'm going to have to deal with conflict and casualties all the time anyway, I might as well make it official!"

Humor is a great way to begin this interview. Not everything we'll hear about will be funny or lighthearted. Not all of Richard's stories will have happy endings. For that matter, they don't all have happy beginnings or cheerful middle sections.

Setting the Stage: A Pastor Prepares

"It was my first assignment and I was excited about it," Richard remembers. "I didn't follow the traditional pathway into pastoral ministry. I didn't go to a Christian college and then head off to seminary to get my master's degree.

"I graduated from high school and then I just worked for a couple of years. College was expensive and I couldn't see any point in spending so much money when I didn't know what I wanted to do with my life. Also, although I was a believer, I wasn't really on fire for God or looking for his direction for my life yet. I believed in God, but I wasn't dedicating my life to him or following closely."

Richard settles more comfortably into his chair.

"It took me a few years before I got serious about God. At that time I was attending [name of church] in [name of city], and week by week the sermons started to get my attention. I began to realize that God might have a plan for my life. And if he did, I wanted to be sure I was centering myself in that plan.

"As I prayed about my life and asked God to guide me, I started sensing that God might want me to go into pastoral ministry. At first I couldn't believe it! I mean at [name of church] we had this amazing pastor, a powerful man of God, and I didn't see any similarity between me and him at all. He was this giant spiritual leader with a powerful ministry, and I was a high-school graduate who didn't go to college and didn't have a life plan.

"Anyway, that's how it all started for me. The more I attended [name of church], the more serious I got about following God. And from there I started praying more, and after that God just made it clear to me that ministry was his path for my life.

"After a lot of prayer, I ended up going to a Bible college with a lot of other adults my age," Richard tells us. "It wasn't the traditional Christian university with all of the students who are eighteen or nineteen years old. When I arrived at the Bible college I was in my mid-twenties, and I was one of the younger students, not one of the older ones.

"I absolutely loved my years at Bible college," Richard sighs. "That was one of the best times of my life. I got squared away with God, I met my wife, I got engaged and then married, and we started our family. For me, all of those major life events happened while I was studying for my degree at Bible college."

Richard smiles broadly.

"I know some people kind of look down on going to a Bible college versus going to an established theological seminary. I get that. But for me, going to Bible college transformed my life. It gave me the tools I needed for ministry. It helped me mature as a person and as a man. It formed me into the kind of godly husband that I needed to be for my wife. Bible college is where I grew up!"

We spend a few minutes talking about dating, engagement, and marriage. Eventually we return to the subject at hand: Richard's experiences of conflict in a local church setting. And for Richard, that begins with what he terms "The battle of the parking lot."

Church Number One: The Battle of the Parking Lot

"A few days after I moved into my office there," Richard remembers, "I dug out a copy of the district journal, which showed the church records. I looked at the pastor before me and he had been there two years. So I looked at the pastor before that, and he had been there for two years. So I looked at the pastor before that, and he had been there a little over three years.

"That startling fact—quick pastoral turnover—hadn't come up when I was learning about the church beforehand. I remember that the superintendent told me about how much money they raised, about the trend in the numbers (stable or flat), and about how nice the parsonage was.

"It was my first assignment and I wasn't smart enough to ask about the recent history, or what I would now call the *pastoral history* of the church. Somehow when I moved into my office, I got curious about that. Who had served there before? How had their experiences gone? Why did they leave? Once I looked at the tenure of my three immediate predecessors, I was suddenly wary about this place.

"I mean, why had three people left so quickly? The town was good-sized; the church was not large but also not tiny. The pay was okay, and the parsonage really was as nice as the superintendent had promised. Let's face it—a lot of guys would feel like they landed in heaven if they were called to this church!

"When I saw all those short tenures of pastoral service, I got very concerned. I wanted to ask someone about it, but I also didn't want to make any waves. So I just kept my mouth shut, and I watched and I listened, and before long I realized why the other guys had run away from this place and ended up going elsewhere."

We are busy taking notes while Richard sorts through his memories.

"What I discovered was that the church was split right down the middle, demographically," he reveals. "Maybe not by demographics in the traditional sense, but I don't know what else to call it. There were two separate types of cultures in the congregation, and the two cultures were truly at war with each other.

"I hadn't seen it during my interview process, which was brief. I hadn't seen it when my wife and I went out there for a weekend, to meet with the key leaders and to look around at the town. Looking back, I wonder how I missed such a sharp clash of cultures, but I really didn't see it in advance. I wish I had! Maybe I would have declined to serve there, or at the very least I would have walked in the door knowing more about what to expect.

"But about the time I was setting up my new office and my wife and I were unpacking into an attractive parsonage, we were starting to get little hints about the culture divide that was separating the church so sharply."

Richard shrugs his shoulders.

"I think I'm just going to be straight with you," he says. "I am going to admit right now, before I even show you the two sides, that in my heart I was on one side of this whole conflict. Although I tried to be impartial and I tried to care for everyone equally, my heart and mind were truly on one side, not the other."

We wait as Richard gathers his thoughts to explain the two sides. "The first side—the side I wasn't on—was composed of long-term church members and church attenders. They were nice people. They were polite on the surface, they put their tithe checks in the offering plate, and they did most of the jobs around the church, including the dirty work of cleaning up or caring for the physical property.

"I am trying to show you their good side first—decent people, good values, hard workers, tithe payers—good folk. But all of them were 'church people,' and they came from long experiences of going to church. They liked their church the way it was, and they really saw themselves as spiritually mature."

Richard exhales loudly.

"I am trying to show you their good side," he repeats. "I am doing my best not to paint these people as monsters. I think underneath all their bad behavior they probably have good hearts. They probably do love God. But they have all been going to church so long that they've lost touch with reality, in my view. They have become 'church people' instead of being 'Christ's people.'

"That distinction—at least to me—is absolutely critical," Richard insists.

"Then there was the other side. Over time, this church had somehow drawn some people out of very rough backgrounds. Knowing what I know now, I would say this church had almost accidentally won some 'Celebrate Recovery' people, and I mean that in a nice way. I love Celebrate Recovery!"

Richard smiles at us.

"This is the group I sided with in my heart," he says. "Saved out of the raw, no manners, not always polite or decent. And to get to the point, some of these people would swear occasionally, although they usually apologized for it later. And they would smoke at church, but only in the parking lot.

"We had these big fellowship dinners once a month, which I actually thought were a pretty good way of reaching the community," Richard recalls. "And if I could show you some videos of those dinners, you would see the two sides very clearly. One group of people is very clean-cut and well-dressed. Even their children are clean-cut and well-dressed.

"The other group of people is rough. They look rough and they talk rough. Some of them are going around the side of the church building to have a smoke. We end up having big piles of cigarette butts in the parking lot, especially on days when we have a fellowship dinner."

Richard smiles at us.

"I am loving that. Absolutely loving it!" he says. "It means we are reaching the right people! It means that even before I got there, this church was reaching the right people. But I have to tell you—I have no idea why those people stayed! It was obvious that they wouldn't really have a place in the church until they totally changed their look and their language. There might as well have been a sign on the wall of the church."

Richard is silent for a moment.

"The first group, the churchy people, held all the political power in the church, or at least all of the elected offices. The second group of people hadn't really gotten organized politically, but they had strong opinions about what our priorities should be as a community of faith. The second group was always pushing for evangelism and outreach and community events, and the first group was always talking about the need to take better care of the building and grounds.

"My sessions with the leadership board quickly devolved into listening to their ongoing complaints about the parking lot, specifically about the trash and the cigarette butts that were littering our parking lot on a regular basis. I saw those things as signs that we were reaching the right kind of people! Our key leaders saw those same things as signs that people weren't surrendered to the Holy Spirit.

"There are probably places and situations where those discussions could be positive and people could find some common ground," Richard continues. "But at this church the two sides were only barely speaking to each other. And somehow I missed that during the interview and the acceptance and preparing to come.

"Once I got there, and once I saw the warfare, I began to believe that God had sent me to be a peacemaker and problem-solver. I waded into it and started calling things the way I saw them."

Richard pauses.

"Or, to put it another way, I guess you could say I started writing the epitaph on my own tombstone—right from the start."

Within only a few weeks of his arrival and installation as pastor, Richard was being drawn into an ongoing tug-of-war between two factions in the church. In his heart he tended to agree with the perspectives of the outreach group. Yet his pay and his core of leaders all derived from the politically powerful group.

Richard believes his ministry was doomed from the beginning.

"I stepped right into it," Richard tells us. "It's like there was this IED buried in the church parking lot and I stepped on it and *boom!* It just blew up.

"My key church leaders saw it this way: If Jesus gets into your life, he starts making you dress up, look like a church person, talk like a church person, think like a church person. If Jesus gets into your life, you immediately stop smoking, quit swearing, and start reading your Bible five hours a day."

Richard stares off into space.

"Okay, I'm exaggerating that a bit," he admits. "But that was the mind-set of the first group. They were glad to have new people come to church, as long as the new people adapted very quickly to a dress-up, holy-looking mind-set. If the new people kept smoking and occasionally let loose with a swear word, that was not okay with the first group. In fact, it seemed to add fuel to their fire.

"Meanwhile, the second group kept reaching out to other people like them, other kind of in-the-rough people, with the result that the second group was growing and the first group was stagnant or declining. I think the first group could see the handwriting on the wall. Eventually the second group was going to have enough votes to get political power in the church and take over.

"So the first group—and I admit this is kind of an assumption on my part—was trying to run off the second group before they became large and in charge."

Richard, whose motives and intentions were positive, found himself drawn into a conflict that soon alienated him from the political powers of the church. He was accused of taking sides and of siding with the outreach crowd. His ideas and suggestions and priorities were not adopted; his attempts to lead or guide the board went absolutely nowhere.

"They would let me show up and preach," Richard sighs. "But in terms of actually leading the church or setting a direction or making a decision, I was frozen out, almost from the beginning. Once they figured out where my heart was, it was clear I would never be allowed to lead or guide the real choices of the church.

"I stayed there long enough that it didn't look like I was running away. And then as soon as I could, I ran away.

"That's exactly what I did.

"I have never said that out loud to anyone, but just saying it right now to you, it rings true to me. That's the core truth of it. I waited until it wouldn't look 'too soon' for an exit, and then I ran for the exit with all my strength. I couldn't find a way to resolve the conflict or bridge the gap or be an unbiased mediator. After looking at it every which way, I couldn't find any answers that suited me.

"I didn't know what to do.

"I ran."

Church Number Two: The Worship Wars

Although we don't necessarily accept Richard's testimony about "running," we do understand what he means. We watch pastors change venues all the time. There is nothing remarkable about this truth: Pastors change venues. What remains unknown, at least to us, is how many of these pastoral transitions are a result of unresolved conflict in the congregation. After trying to solve the problem, or perhaps after deciding that he or she is part of the problem, the pastor looks for greener pastures. The pastor moves on; the problem stays right where it is.

At least in Richard's case, he landed well in his next assignment.

He was young, and then as now physically fit and personally charismatic. Once upon a time the Israelites wanted a king and preferred a tall one with a commanding presence. In these current days, God's people are much the same. When they seek a leader they tend to look with human eyes and choose with natural (versus spiritual) understanding. An attractive, fit, younger pastoral prospect will always find it easier to get a new assignment when compared with an older, less fit, less attractive potential candidate.

Among the people of God we might wish for a process saturated with prayer and blind to trivial, surface issues like someone's personal appearance or stature. These wishes, now as in the days of King Saul, might fail to get much traction. People like what they like, and they tend to like their pastors young, attractive, and if possible with a few adorable children at home. (Adding a golden retriever and a fireplace would be a nice touch.)

Richard ended up moving to one of the "flagship" churches of a certain district of his denomination. In each venue or jurisdiction there are a handful of churches whose revenues pay the broader budgets and whose size places them in the upper tier among churches in the region. Richard moved to a church like this: a place of some prominence. Although his pastoral history to that point was brief, there were no serious mistakes and no visible issues popping out on his résumé. Instead there was a young, attractive pastor whose first church had seemed to go okay, who now was looking to move up in the world and take a larger assignment.

A larger assignment is exactly what Richard took, and gladly so.

"Things went well," Richard says without any trace of boasting or pride. "We followed a semi-retired guy who had let things get kind of stagnant. The church was holding on and was very solid financially, but not much was happening overall. Somehow when I got there everything just kind of rumbled into life and the engines of the church really started to hum.

"I wasn't taking credit for any of that at the time, and I certainly don't take credit for it now," Richard claims. "I think it was just a case where some new blood breathes new life into a group of people. I came in and started preaching a sermon series I had used in my previous church. But where in the previous church I had gotten only a lukewarm reaction, all of a sudden I was getting loud "Amens!" and visible signs of approval while I was preaching. I don't think I actually *was* a better preacher, but after moving to [name of second church] I quickly *felt* like a better preacher."

Richard takes a moment to talk to us about the numbers and statistics, which surged upward after his arrival. Very quickly his church was at the top of the charts in its local district, getting awards at assembly and winning the young pastor a sense of accomplishment and achievement.

"Things were going well," is how Richard remembers the season. "I was enjoying preaching, and there weren't any big problems to solve. Looking back I should have left well enough alone. Instead, I began to feel like people were ready to follow my leadership, so I decided that I would try some leading.

"I started with our worship experience, which proved to be a big mistake."

Richard pauses here, and despite ourselves we reflect on countless places and a large number of churches in which worship style has proved to be a stubborn and at times intractable area of conflict. Time after time we've watched churches break apart or encounter serious trauma in a tug-of-war battle over what kind of worship was going to happen on Sunday mornings.

"Our worship leader at the time was a guy I inherited from the previous pastor," Richard tells us. "In fact, he was actually related by marriage to the previous pastor, and the two of them had been really close.

"When I got there, I already knew that. But I didn't see any reason to get rid of the guy, or even try to encourage him to leave. I liked his personality and I also enjoyed the way he led our worship services. I didn't come in with any agenda to change worship. I didn't come in with any agenda to change personnel.

"But after I'd been there a while, and with my preaching seeming to go so well, I decided I would like to upgrade our worship experience. We were having hymns on Sunday and some praise choruses too, but nothing lively or interesting, nothing like a worship team or a praise band or anywhere close to that.

"If you grew up in a fairly conservative church, our worship style was a great fit for you," Richard relates. "We had a core of people who had grown up in churches just like ours. Some of them had grown up in our church, and they liked worship the way it had always been. Sing through a few hymns, mix in a few praise choruses, and we're done. No guitars, no drums, no team of three or four people leading worship from the platform. Nothing like that at all.

"I decided to upgrade our worship experience, and before I even got started with doing that, I was in big trouble.

"Before doing anything else, I confided in our worship leader that I wanted to move our services in a more contemporary direction. I told him I wanted to consider adding in one or two more voices on the platform and that sometimes I would like to have us try a band onstage—maybe guitar or trumpet, and maybe at times also a drummer.

"The guy nodded and seemed to go along with me. He didn't argue with me or complain about my direction. In fact, he seemed to get it. I actually ended my meeting with him believing that we were both on the same page.

"But what really happened was the minute that our meeting was over, my worship leader got on the phone to a few key friends and allies in the congregation. He blew everything all out of proportion immediately. He told people that the pastor had decided to radically change our worship style, and that soon we were going to be having drums on the platform. He told them we'd soon hear loud rock music playing in the sanctuary every Sunday."

Richard's voice trails off quietly.

"I am still wounded by that disloyalty and that falsehood," Richard admits. "We sat together, we talked together, and this guy never raised even a slight objection to what I was saying. And here I was just talking theoretical possibilities and trying to get his reaction to possible change. I hadn't made any big decisions yet, and I certainly wasn't trying to change [name of second church] into a full-blown Hard Rock Café every Sunday!"

Richard frowns, adrift in his memories.

"He was on the phone within ten minutes of talking to me. He called all of his friends, most of whom served on our leader board. He had a firestorm brewing before I was even in my car and going home from our meeting. Before I knew it, the topic of worship style was on the agenda for our next board meeting, and there was vile gossip spreading out in all directions, contaminating the whole church."

Richard pauses.

"Ironically, that gossip cut both ways," he says with a wry smile. "When some people got wind of that, they were actually encouraged that our church might try to break out and become contemporary. But when others heard it, they were outraged and they decided that I was a dangerous, unstable, loose cannon of a pastor."

Again Richard is silent.

"How could I have handled that differently?" Richard asks rhetorically. "I sat down with the person who would be most affected—our worship leader—and I just had a quiet talk with him about *possibilities*—not decisions. And I was very clear in our conversation that I was talking about trying a few small, incremental changes. I was *not* advocating a radical overhaul of the way we did worship."

Richard looks at us, assessing our reaction.

"I was betrayed," he says. "Maybe that sounds melodramatic to you, but that's how it felt and that's how it still looks to me, when I look back on it from a distance. By trying to be fair, and trying to be inclusive of a staff member that I inherited, I ended up losing control of a church-wide conversation about how we wanted to do worship on Sunday mornings.

"By the time the next board meeting happened, people were angry and ready to pass motions that would ban guitars and drums from our platform for eternity. A few people were ready to ban their pastor from the platform too!"

Although Richard made good-faith efforts to calm the situation, and although he attempted to re-clarify his original remarks to his staff member, the size and scope of the lie had already changed the landscape of Richard's pastoral service. One minute Richard was enjoying a positive response to his preaching, and in the next moment he was preaching to people who wouldn't make eye contact with him, wouldn't return his phone calls, and wouldn't engage in simple conversation in the hallways of the church.

"We went into battle mode immediately," Richard says as he describes the church and its response to the rumors. "I tried to be a mediator and a calm leader. I did my best to get the truth out and let it breathe. But honestly, the truth never had a chance. The lie was already out there and already believed. Every time I insisted that I had been talking about possible changes, and small changes and only that, everyone assumed I was lying.

"My leadership was undermined and undone in an instant," is how Richard sizes up the situation, now viewing it from a safe distance and a successful new career in the military.

"I'll tell you one thing," Richard says later. "I value ideas like chain of command and obeying superior officers. Here in the military things are just crystal-clear about who's in charge and why it matters. I may not always agree with the ideas happening above me, but you can bet I salute and carry out my orders."

Richard pauses.

"And you can also bet that I don't spread lies behind the back of the man I report to, and I don't start rumors about some new policy coming to our base. There is a unity and a camaraderie in the military that I never found in my two churches. Maybe it's just me, but I love having a clear chain of command, and I love the unity of all of us following orders and doing our duty."

Can you relate to what Richard is saying here?

Questions for Reflection

Pastors and Ministers

1. If you moved to a new assignment and inherited a worship leader who was related to the previous pastor, would you release him or her from service immediately? Or would you take a wait-and-see approach such as Richard took in his second assignment? With the advantage of hindsight in Richard's specific case, do you believe he would have been wiser to release the worship leader right from the start and bring in a new staff person?

2. Have you ever watched a pastor successfully (i.e., with little or no conflict and with seemingly good outcomes) transform the worship experience of a church from one style to another? If you've seen this happen, why do you believe the outcome was successful?

3. Have you ever had to risk opposing the views or priorities of those who held the political and financial power in your congregation? Did you believe that you were jeopardizing your continued employment if you expressed a different opinion or pursued a different priority?

4. If you had to choose, would you say that "pastoral bravery" or "pastoral compliance" is a wiser strategy for those who serve in ministry to local congregations? Which character trait—brave in the face of adversity or compliant with the wishes of those who are in power—do you personally favor as the wiser choice?

5. If you are old enough to believe that your future options for pastoral employment might be somewhat limited, would this affect your level of "bravery" in a given situation? Would you be more likely to go along with those in power in order to keep your job? To what extent, if any,

does your age and perceived employability affect the way in which you interact with the financial and political powers within your church?

Local Churches and Church Boards

1. If an outsider were looking at your congregation, would he or she describe you as being a "conflicted" or "divided" church? Why or why not?

2. In your view, how should church conflict be resolved? Is it the primary responsibility of the different factions to come together and make peace? Is it the pastor's responsibility to serve as a referee, helping the two sides "play fair" and come to agreement? Should the local denominational leader get involved and lead the factions through some kind of formal process of resolving conflicts? Who bears the primary responsibility for this?

3. How often have you watched a serious conflict in the church be fully and positively resolved? How often have you seen clashing or opposite church factions come together in unity, resolve their differences, and then work together in harmony toward mutually agreed priorities? If you have seen this happen, reflect on how and why this outcome was achieved.

4. How often have you watched a church split, or how often have you seen a sizable faction or group leave the church and go elsewhere? In your view, is this type of exodus inevitable? If people are opposed to a pastor or a set of priorities or another faction within the church, should these people leave and find some other church?

Denominational Leaders

1. To what extent are you aware of the political dynamics of the many congregations under your care? Do you make an effort to discern the hidden or internal political structures in each location, or do you wait until some issue or some emerging conflict discloses the political structure?

2. If you were personally aware of a "divided" church that was separated into warring factions, would you disclose this fact to a prospective pastoral candidate? Why or why not? What would be your own rationale for giving this information to, or withholding it from, an incoming minister?

3. Within your own denominational tradition, who bears the primary responsibility for peacemaking with regard to the existence of conflict in a local congregation? Is the pastor expected to be the ultimate peacemaker and problem-solver? Are you as the presiding denominational leader expected to serve the peacemaking role? Who bears the primary responsibility for working through congregational conflict and birthing the structures and practices of future congregational health?

4. If you knew of a conflicted or divided congregation, would you be likely to seek a young and untested pastoral candidate or a more experienced pastor who had endured trials and tribulations in his or her career? Would you, like the district superintendent in this specific case, have knowingly sent a pastor with no prior experience into a setting with this type of dynamics?

EIGHT

M*A*S*H

WHEN PASTORS ARE AMONG THE WOUNDED

Leaders arrive to serve us with every kind of temperament and personality. Some great leaders are brash and bold while other excellent managers tend to be quiet and contemplative. There is no single pastoral "type" or temperament. The men and women who minister to us as pastors represent the full spectrum of human personalities and characteristics.

Because leaders can vary so dramatically by temperament and perspective, there is no one single way in which a pastor or leader responds to being hurt in a congregational conflict. Pastors with a thicker skin may move triumphantly from one conflict to the next, seemingly unscathed by the traumas of battle. Leaders with a more sensitive nature may be deeply harmed by words or situations that seem relatively minor to others. Sometimes the damage is visible on the surface; we can tell when we're dealing with a wounded leader. At other times the damage from church conflict may be subsumed by other issues, only to emerge much later in a seemingly unrelated situation or circumstance. Since leaders are all different, trauma and conflict affects leaders in different ways.

The psalmist David, whose journey took him from shepherd to soldier to king, has left us in Scripture an amazing journal about serving in leadership—the trials and tribulations, the joys and rewards. David made mistakes as every leader does; David also dealt with frustrating leadership challenges such as betrayal, disloyalty, and rebellion. His story arcs across a full spectrum of difficult situations; his psalms show us the inner workings of his emotions.

There is a self-revealing quality to David's work. If he were alive today he might be blogging, and many of us might subscribe to his posts. The transparency of many of David's psalms helps us relate to the author and his world. We, too, have struggled to control our emotions. We, too, have come home exhausted and defeated after a major conflict, perhaps wishing to die or be done with it.

In Psalm 109 David writes "my heart is wounded within me" (v. 22). What pastor hasn't experienced times like these, when in the midst of serving faithfully and being obedient to the calling, he or she is attacked or accused or betrayed? The sheer unfairness of the situation can elevate and intensify feelings of despair and withdrawal, resentment and rage.

Pastors get hurt.

Pastors get tired of being hurt.

Pastors leave the ministry.

The Wounded Warrior Project

Walter and Susan arrived at their new parsonage feeling worn out. Power struggles and conflict at their previous church had dragged on for months, long enough that the entire pastoral family felt wounded from the many battles. With two school-age children to manage and with a third child on the way, Susan was ready to raise her family in an environment that was calm and peaceful. Susan was urging for change and Walter was worn out from fighting, so they looked around for a while until a new opportunity finally opened up, two states away.

By their own descriptions, they arrived feeling worn out and exhausted. Susan was too weary to look for work; her pregnancy was not going well, and she often had physical issues to cope with. Walter felt depleted both emotionally and spiritually; he wasn't sure he could preach well in the new place.

"I had very little to offer," is Walter's description of his condition as he arrived to serve in a new parish. "To use a battery analogy, I felt like my battery was not just low—it was completely run down. I knew I needed recharging, but when and where is that actually an option for worn-out ministers? I mean, maybe if we'd had six or eight months between churches to just renew and refresh ourselves, that might have made it a completely different experience.

"Instead, I just moved my exhausted self from one place to another."

A well-organized Bible student and passionate scholar, Walter had kept meticulous notes from his previous sermons, including messages he had preached while in college and seminary. He had amassed a computer database of more than 150 of his previous sermons, so on arriving at the new community he made no effort to hash out some new material. Instead, he culled out some of the sermons he liked best from among his existing inventory and preached his way through material he had already written.

"Recycling," Walter says with a wry smile. "Isn't that supposed to be good for the environment?"

Preaching through old material may seem like a wise choice, given the low energy Walter was experiencing. However, by failing to energize and activate his mental interest, the recycled sermons only contributed to his general sense of malaise and weariness. He found himself bored with ministry, tired of listening to other people's problems, and daydreaming about other kinds of jobs.

"I earned my paychecks there," Walter insists in retrospect. "I did my calling; I was faithful in hospital visits. I preached my sermons, and I led all of the meetings. I met all the criteria of what they expected and deserved from a pastor, but I was only going through the motions. My heart wasn't in it. How much that was visible to people I don't know.

"Susan knew I was phoning it in, and I knew it too. Beyond that, I don't know how perceptive people were. I'd like to think that my recycled sermons were pretty good, so maybe no one noticed that I was personally disinterested in what I was preaching.

"Did I just say that out loud? I can't believe I said that to you."

Walter pauses to reflect.

"For me," he continues later, "my mantra has always been that if I'm not interested in a message, why should the audience care? So I have tried to study and preach about things that are interesting to me, things I am passionate about.

"When I got there [to the third and final church assignment], I couldn't find the energy to study anything or develop any new series. I just preached through my old material, sometimes almost verbatim. My kids were so young they didn't notice, so only Susan and I knew what was really going on.

"The whole time I served [name of church] there was a little voice in my head, telling me that I was cheating these people out of the leadership they deserved from me. There was this little accusing voice in my head—I am not trying to suggest anything supernatural here—that just kept telling me I should quit, I should give up, I should get out of the way and let this church choose the kind of pastor they needed and deserved.

"I was thirty-two at that time," Walter remembers, "but functionally I felt like maybe a seventy- or eighty-year-old pastor. I felt like I was coming to the end of my life's service, and I was just going through the motions. I was just waiting for the buzzer to sound or the whistle to blow, so that I could punch the time clock and go home."

Walter is silent.

"We stayed more than a year," he says quietly. "And then the voice in my head finally won. I called the superintendent and told him I would serve there until he could find a replacement. He was surprised but I think he could tell my mind was made up. The only favor I asked him was if he could find someone quickly. I told him that I would honor my commitment—I would stay until he found someone else to serve—but I also asked him to find someone quickly.

"He found someone in a couple of months. He came over and joined me for a board meeting and I announced my resignation to the board. They were all very surprised. I think at first they thought there had been a moral failure or something, either mine or Susan's. Eventually they realized I was just tired and wanted out.

"To their credit a couple of guys on my board actually tried to talk me out of it. They told me my ministry was effective and they valued my leadership. I wish they had talked like that a little earlier! I don't know if it would have changed anything, but when I already had one foot out the door, they told me my leadership was effective. They told me they liked my preaching. They told me they were sorry to see me go."

Walter shrugs.

"Would I still be a pastor today if they had talked to me sooner?" he asks rhetorically. "I really don't know the answer to that. By the time I got some positive feedback from my primary board members, I had already made up my mind."

Walter sighs and looks at us across the table.

"I don't think my story is dramatic enough for your book," he tells us. "There should be fireworks or major trauma or something. The truth is kind of anticlimactic in our case. Susan and I were both worn out from all the conflict in our previous setting, and we came to the new ministry exhausted. So even though there wasn't any conflict in the church we came to serve, I ended up leaving the ministry.

"That's not fair to [final place of service]," he admits. "My departure from serving in ministry certainly wasn't their fault. It wasn't an indictment of their leadership or their conduct or anything else. It wasn't about them at all.

"I just came into that setting very beat up and very exhausted, and nothing happened there that ever turned me around," he says slowly. "I didn't get recharged in any way while I served there. Simply going through the motions didn't get me revved up or excited again. I was there for two cycles of both Mother's Day and Fourth of July messages, plus I had two Lenten seasons, two Easter Sundays, and one Advent and Christmas. All of those big events on the calendar didn't give me more energy or make me feel inspired. I pulled out some previous messages for all of those times, and all the other Sundays too. I just served my time, kind of watched the clock, and felt like a fraud. Ministry was happening, and some of it was effective, but my heart wasn't in it."

Walter settles back in his chair.

"Am I still called to ministry?" he wonders. "I ask myself that question on a regular basis. I'm in a different place now, emotionally, so maybe I could handle being back in the pastorate again. But I'm happy in my current job, Susan loves our current home, and my kids are in good schools. Not to mention I'm making probably double what I would earn at most churches where I might serve.

"For me," he says, "I think ministry is a closed chapter of my life. I wish things had gone differently for me, for Susan, and for our kids. I got so beat up at [name of church] that even after I left there, I couldn't find a heart for ministry any more. Nothing felt authentic inside me; mostly I felt broken and lost."

When No One Will Follow

Is it possible for a pastor to look too young or sound too young or perhaps even be too young to be effective?

"Don't let anyone look down on you because you are young," Paul writes to Timothy (1 Timothy 4:12). Paul goes on to suggest that the best defense against such disrespect is to "set an example for the believers in speech, in conduct, in love, in faith and in purity."

Garrett believed he was following that advice as he entered his first pastorate. At twenty-four years old he was a graduate of a respected Christian university and had a master's degree from a seminary that was within the theological traditions of his own denomination. His grades in both schools were exemplary; he had been active in ministry even as a student.

"I got my BA when I was twenty-one," Garrett relates. "I was twenty-four when I finished my MDiv program. I had a couple of interviews during my final year of seminary, then had a couple of job offers to consider. Based on my grades and my experiences and my references, I had two churches both wanting to hire me.

"Please forgive me if it sounds like I'm boasting, or if this seems self-serving. I am just trying to paint the picture for you. I did a little bit of preaching while I was still in college; during seminary I did quite a bit of preaching. Whenever I preached it seemed to go well; there was good response.

"I married Val and she was a warm, charming, beautiful, godly woman," Garrett smiles. "I mean, she added so much to my life and my ministry! She was everything you'd want a pastor's wife to be. She had a heart for God, a heart for other people, and she was just an outgoing, warm, very social person."

In Garrett's view, the couple's future looked bright.

Given the wonderful situation of being wanted by two churches, Garrett and Valerie took their time, prayed a lot, and sought wise counsel. Eventually they said yes to a church in a prosperous suburb of a large city. The church wasn't large, but it was very solid financially and had a rich history within the denomination. Many future leaders had passed through this specific church en route to future successes. A handful of former denominational leaders had retired in the area and now attended the church, adding allure to the prospect of serving there.

Garrett and Valerie began their pastoral service less than two months after graduation, after a short break during which they traveled, visited friends and family, and made plans for their move. Then, with high hopes and great expectations, they packed up a truck and departed for their first assignment in ministry.

As you might guess from its inclusion in this chapter, Garrett's first place of ministry was also his last. Yet there was no moral failure, no traumatic conflict in the church, no especially thorny issue or problem that derailed the career of a bright young preacher who seemed destined for better days. Instead, Garrett's career ended because, by his own admission, he never achieved respect in his place of ministry. Perhaps, he believes, because he looked and sounded too young to be taken seriously.

"The church had this whole history of great leaders and pastors," Garrett remembers. "They had one wall out in the foyer that was kind of a pantheon of past leaders—all these impressive framed pictures of pastors and missionaries and other leaders who had either served this church or had come from this church as they moved out into places of service.

"As I told you before, we had retired leaders attending the church. In fact, there was kind of a 'gray hair cluster' of retired ministers, most of them having held high office in the church. I was excited about that when I was called to pastor there, because I saw it, at least in part, as their vote of confidence in me."

Garrett stares off into space for a moment.

"When I got there, it was all much different than I expected," he relates. "Maybe I had unrealistic expectations about what pastoring was going to be. Maybe my work in college and seminary had given me an exaggerated sense of my own gifts. But whatever the reason, I hit a wall almost immediately."

Garrett pauses to frame his thoughts more clearly.

"My preaching went well," he tells us. "There was very good response to my preaching. I would stand at the back of the sanctuary on Sundays, with Valerie at my side, and people would walk by and tell me how much they had enjoyed my message that day. The 'gray hair cluster' was always among those who would stop and tell me they enjoyed the message.

"I felt valued, I felt included, I felt liked," Garrett says. "And for a short time that was enough. But what I noticed almost immediately was that anytime I tried to actually lead the church—point us in a direction, establish a priority for us, set a tone for how we might approach something—it just didn't get any traction at all. Whenever I tried to lead in that kind of way, I was politely ignored."

Garrett stops his narrative and looks at us intently.

"Believe me, there is nothing polite about ignoring your pastor," he says quietly but firmly. "Every time I tried to take some leadership in how we might celebrate the seasons of Advent or Lent or how we might do something charitable out in the broader community or anything like that, I was just ignored. People on the board would nod their heads and let me talk as much as I wanted to, but then they wouldn't move forward in the direction I was trying to take us.

"Although the 'gray hair cluster' wasn't among the board (with one exception), they did manage to control the board, and they also managed to control the church. I'm not saying that they were evil, or they were bad people, or even that they had wrong motives. I am talking about some of the most famous people in our tradition! I'm sure they are absolutely wonderful—they are probably better saints than I am.

"But they had a stranglehold on that congregation, and they weren't about to let go of it—at least not for a young pastor starting out. So from my perspective they hired me to look good in public and sound good in the pulpit, but behind the scenes they wanted to control the church in pretty much every aspect of its life. Does this sound cynical or sarcastic? I don't mean to sound that way, I really don't. Judging only by their behavior, the true leaders of this church were happy to let me stand up and preach but completely unwilling to let me stand up and lead.

"Other than the fact that I was only twenty-four years old, I don't know what else might have been the problem," Garrett speculates. "I didn't get into trouble with any of them, and even on my last Sunday there I had people coming up to tell me how great my message was and how much they were going to miss me."

After roughly eighteen months of getting no respect for his leadership, Garrett decided he wasn't willing to be the "pretty face" of ministry unless he was also the person who set the tone, established the direction, and led the priorities and the mission of the church. He was not comfortable with an "only preaching" mind-set. After all, he believed he had been hired to lead.

After prayerfully talking things over with Val, Garrett set out three major priorities that he believed in with all of his heart. After several long talks with Val, and after a particularly long and helpful conversation with Val's parents, Garrett decided that if the board and the church wouldn't sign on to his three priorities when he presented them, he would step down from his role as pastor.

Four months after Garrett and Valerie came to that decision together, Garrett did in fact submit his resignation. After sharing his three priorities with the board, and after much urging (on his part) to get a hearing on moving the church in these directions with regard to ministry, the board declined to go along.

"I wasn't taking us over a cliff," Garrett says as he looks back at that time in his ministry. "If you looked at my three priorities, they were things that almost any seminary at the time would have been teaching and recommending. I was in line with current ecclesiological thinking at that time, and it's still current now. I was not being a rebel or being a contrarian or anything else. I was simply trying to point the church in the direction of meaningful, fruitful, effective ministry."

Despite what Garrett describes as his best efforts, the board and leaders would not be moved. While he waited for the outcome to emerge, Garrett talked with his wife about possible next steps.

Twenty-two months after accepting his first pastoral assignment, Garrett preached his last sermon, packed up his books and belongings, and vacated his office at the church. He accepted a mid-level management job at a commodities trading firm in another city. Within two years the title on his business card said "Executive Vice President" and Garrett was earning more than four times as much per year as his pastoral salary had been.

"If I was honest with you—and I am trying to be—I would tell you that I wish I was still a pastor there," Garrett says wistfully. "Pretty much all my life I saw my future as being in ministry. I would love to have served that church for thirty or forty years and led us together as a faith community toward some great goals.

"All of that is a lot more meaningful than what I'm doing now," he says with a trace of remorse in his voice. "That matters for eternity. So maybe someday I'll get back into that line of work. But for now I have to tell you, I am respected at work, and my opinion is valued, and my contributions are making a difference, every day.

"I get paid a lot here but the bigger and better thing is that I am respected here and listened to here. People follow my leadership here.

"You can't put a dollar sign on that," Garrett claims. "It's priceless."

Verily, Thus Saith the Board

In this second decade of the twenty-first century, it might surprise some readers to discover that there are congregations scattered across North America that are still firmly resisting many forms of our contemporary culture, including contemporary Christian culture. In these sanctuaries and spaces, no one is leading worship using songs or choruses written by Matt Redman, Hillsong, or Michael W. Smith. No one is praising God by singing a song that was written in the past three or four decades; instead, the music material is much older and far more traditional.

In some of these same places there is a reverence for the King James Version of the Bible that some believe may border on idolatry. The only trustworthy and reliable translation of the Holy Scriptures, according to those in these places, can be found in translation work that is more than half a millennia old, using source documents that predate literally thousands of recent discoveries. They believe the only way to faithfully proclaim the Holy Scriptures is to use the archaic version of English that was in vogue more than five centuries ago.

Are there really such places? We are not talking here about anecdotal stories that may have been blown out of proportion. We are not discussing some rumor from the Internet or a blog from the wackysphere. There are real congregations, composed of real people, who do not sing praise choruses and who do not read Bibles unless the cover assures them that the translation was commissioned by King James, crowned ruler of the old British Empire.

Mason was being driven to one of these places, and his presiding bishop was describing the nature of the congregation, including their preferences about which Scriptures might be read in their services. To Mason, these people sounded quaint and perhaps sentimental. He had an almost fond regard for their isolated and culturally backward (from his view) perspective. He thought of them (having not yet met them) as perhaps another version of today's Amish populations.

The bishop was clear. Among the few "absolutes" that the congregation had proclaimed was this one: Their new minister must use the King James—and *only* the King James—in all sermons and services. There was no room for other, more recent translations. The sermons and services were to be all King James, all the time, no exceptions.

The bishop may not have agreed with this perspective (he wisely kept his thoughts to himself), but the bishop was very clear with the candidate. Mason was informed of this "absolute" in the very first conversation he had with the man who would be his presiding supervisor. Mason was intrigued by the charm of this quaint custom; he did not feel particularly offended by it. Instead, he saw himself as the leader who might gently pry this fearful, backward-facing congregation into the sunny light of contemporary, authentic biblical scholarship and learning.

Mason, a very bright student, even believed that perhaps God had prepared him "for such a time as this"—an assignment to lead this group into modernity. He was relaxed about meeting the leader board, and he approached the meeting with a mixture of intellectual curiosity and personal warmth. What if the Amish invited you over to one of their communities to have a look around? Mason approached his interview process with this type of mind-set. He was a tourist, looking forward to hiking a terrain that was entirely unfamiliar to him but quite interesting.

The interview went well. Although the bishop had the full authority to simply install Mason as pastor, the bishop wisely (he was not a bishop for nothing) tended to involve the key leaders in the pastoral search process. He did so in most cases, not all, but in this case it seemed especially prudent. It is not easy to find recent seminary graduates who are willing to dust off a King James Bible. It is not simple to find aspiring pastors who want to preach as if the Dead Sea

Scrolls and literally thousands of other Scripture fragments had never been pried out of their caves and catacombs in the Middle East.

Mason was welcomed by the prospective congregation, right from the start. The interview went very well. Unknown to Mason, he was the third candidate that the wise old bishop had driven to this place—the other two having failed the test of "King James only"—and by failing that particular test had failed also to gain any traction with the leaders.

Mason's disarming smile and his willing embrace of the King James issue brought him immediate acclaim. The leaders smiled, the bishop smiled, Mason smiled, and the arrangement was complete. Mason began his service to the group a few weeks later, driving to the community with his young wife and a small trailer load of their possessions, mostly books.

Setting up his new office, Mason envisioned his role as a champion of Scripture, almost as a Wycliffe translator coming to a new tribe. He would speak the language of these people—he would use it willingly, just as they insisted—but meanwhile he would also translate the archaic language of King James into the vernacular and common language of the day. If he had to preach from the King James this was not a major issue; he could start there, and then explain what the king's own translators were trying to faithfully communicate.

Mason was excited about his assignment.

His excitement lasted all the way into week three, just after his third Sunday of preaching to the congregation. After a sermon that went well (he believed) he was met at the back door by one of the key leaders.

"Good sermon, pastor," the leader began, receiving a warm smile from Mason in return. "But one thing. None of us like the part where you start explaining the Scripture and trying to change what it means. We're not okay with that. We want God's language and

God's ways around here. We do not want the language of man or the ways of man. We especially do not want that from the pulpit!"

With that terse comment, and without any further elaboration, the lay leader excused himself and walked out the church door.

Mason, like an expectant Mary awaiting the birth of Christ, "kept all these things, and pondered them in [his] heart" (Luke 2:19, KJV). It was a warning shot, fired at a very unexpected moment, but Mason was not yet greatly concerned. He went back over his mental notes of the message, wondering where or how he had ventured into anything that might be regarded as heresy.

He had not done so. After a thorough review, he was sure of that.

Over lunch at home, Mason and his bride discussed the matter.

"Sherry was a lot more worried about it than I was," Mason remembers. "She felt like it might really mean something. Like it might be an important comment with some hidden meanings behind it.

"I listened to her because I love her, but I really didn't think it was a big deal. My view was that I had somehow said something that offended a specific person, and the specific person (that particular leader) had simply complained a bit. I made a mental note to be nice to that guy, but after reviewing my mental notes of the sermon, I was confident that I had been orthodox, accurate, and entirely faithful to the true meaning of the Holy Scriptures.

"And I had read those Scriptures to them in the King James, as required!"

Mason pauses.

"That happened eight years ago," he muses. "And for the record, it wasn't the first time my wife was right about something! Her intuition was a lot more plugged in than mine was. Even after getting a brief scolding from that specific person, I didn't see a larger problem or a bigger issue. I thought a grumpy guy got something off his chest and blew off some steam with the pastor—no big deal.

"I was entirely wrong about that."

Two Sundays later, after another message that Mason believed had gone very well, he was approached by the same lay leader.

"We're having a meeting on Tuesday night, here at the church," the leader told him. "And we need you to be there."

When Mason asked about the content or purpose of the meeting, the leader merely shrugged.

"Be there, and be on time," Mason was told.

At this point Mason did begin to worry a bit, and his wife was in full panic. Only five sermons into his first assignment and Mason was being summoned to a meeting that he had not called, that he would not lead, and that he did not even know the purpose of.

Looking back, he made one key mistake that he would change if he could.

"I didn't call my bishop," Mason says, looking glum. "I mean, the guy had just installed me a few weeks earlier! It was way too soon to go running to him with a big problem or to be complaining to him about anything.

"My attitude was that I needed to 'man up' and deal with it, and get it over with, whatever it was. Strange as it seems, I didn't immediately connect the dots. I didn't realize that my alleged meddling with Scripture was going to be the issue."

At the hastily-called meeting, four separate elders of the church spoke out. Each one of the men delivered approximately the same message to their newly installed pastor. As Mason remembers it, each lay leader told him, "We hired you to *proclaim* the Scriptures; we do not want you to *explain* the Scriptures. We want to keep everything just the way God said it—no interpreting."

By Mason's account of that meeting, he tried to explain himself and he tried to let the leaders know that the whole point of a sermon is to explore Scripture, to tell God's people what God's Word means to them in their own daily lives. Yet the more Mason spoke, the more tension built in the room.

"I was probably a bit defensive," Mason says, "but I didn't get angry. I was honestly trying to explain to these guys that the whole point of writing a sermon is to take the Scripture—what God says—and then explain and apply that truth to the situations we face every day in our own lives.

"But the more I explained that idea—or tried to—the angrier people got."

After repeated efforts by the young pastor to simply explain the purpose of preaching the Scripture, the meeting went from tense and angry to an almost eerie silence and quietness. Mason, for his part, had exhausted himself trying to explain the art and purpose of sermons and preaching.

The key lay leader—the man who had talked to Mason after week three—then simply said, "If you can't keep to *proclaiming* the Scripture, and if you insist that you are going to be *explaining* the Scripture, then we are going to the bishop and getting you moved to another place."

Mason had no response to that.

He called the bishop after the meeting and was surprised to hear that the bishop was already aware of the situation.

"What would you like to do?" Mason recalls the bishop asking him.

"I honestly have no idea," Mason confessed to his supervisor. "How on earth am I supposed to preach without preaching?"

After further discussion the bishop advised Mason to submit his resignation, announce a departure date from the church and—if the leaders would allow—go ahead and preach for another two or three weeks until his departure. Although Mason and the bishop agreed to this proposal, the lay leaders were not willing to allow Mason another chance in the pulpit—unless he would "only read" and "not try to explain" the Scriptures.

Mason refused this condition on principle, and never preached again for that congregation. He remained in the parsonage for another few weeks. Then he and his wife packed their few belongings, rented a moving truck, and were back on the highway just two months after arriving to serve in this place.

The bishop, who saw Mason as a useful and talented young minister, offered two other potential places of service. Meanwhile Mason, confused and disoriented, reached out to a former professor and was offered a teaching fellowship at his former seminary. He could work on a further graduate degree while doing some teaching and assisting his former professor.

For Mason, it was the right fit at the right time.

In the eight years since his fateful encounter with the small church, Mason has neither sought nor accepted another pastoral assignment.

"I use that experience as a case study in one of the courses I teach," Mason says with a slight smile. "I don't identify the geographic location or the name of the church, but I use that congregation and its leaders as an example of how *not* to approach the Holy Scriptures."

Will he ever pastor again?

Mason does not hesitate.

"I've found my niche here," he says brightly. "I love teaching. I love studying God's Word in the original languages—not English—and I love helping students unpack the meaning of the Scriptures with accuracy and insight.

"I can't imagine why I would ever subject myself to the whims and wishes of people who won't even study and learn," he says simply. "That is a denial of everything I stand for, and everything I'm trying to do with my life."

Questions for Reflection

Pastors and Ministers

1. Think back to the story of Walter. Are there situations or circumstances in which a burnt-out pastor should remain in his or her current assignment (the setting of the burnout) or is it always wiser to remove burnt-out ministers from their current roles?

2. Should a superintendent or bishop assess the "emotional health" or "energy level" of a pastoral candidate before installing him or her in a new place? What kind of evaluation would/should that involve?

3. Should Walter have been sent to some sort of "pastoral rehab" before being plopped into a new pulpit? Are such resources available somewhere? Do you personally know where to find pastoral renewal and/or rehabilitation at the deep level of soul and spiritual refreshment?

4. Since the preaching was going well in Garrett's situation, should he have been content to preach and be the public figurehead of the congregation? By all accounts he might have done so almost forever because people liked his preaching. Should he have hung around longer as the preacher, hoping to gain political traction later on? Why or why not? If you would advise him to wait around and build some political currency, about how long should he expect to wait?

5. Consider Mason's situation, in which the congregation was focused on the King James Version of the Bible. If you were a bishop, would you comply with the wishes of a group like this and continue to search for persons who would "read" but not "teach" and who would read only from one specific approved translation? Why or why not?

6. Should seminaries teach more courses in group dynamics, managing change, and coping with cultural dynamics in a congregation?

Local Churches and Church Boards

1. Has it ever occurred to you to evaluate or consider the spiritual, emotional, and/or physical health of a potential pastoral candidate who might serve your congregation? Do you expect or believe that the district superintendent, bishop, or other presiding official has already done this type of monitoring of these core health issues for all candidates? Who, if anyone, is responsible to determine or assess the health of a person who might become your next pastor?

2. Is it your practice to invite a prospective candidate to come out and meet the leaders, preach for the congregation, and interact with the board? If so, what do you hope to discover about a candidate during this process? Are you looking for someone who is strong in the pulpit (preaches well) or does your search include and focus on less tangible issues, such as the emotional health, physical health, or spiritual health of the candidate?

3. Has it ever occurred to you that every pastor is fundamentally human, and that he or she may be in the process of becoming mature, rather than already having arrived at that destination? Would your congregation be a safe and positive place for someone to "grow up" emotionally and even spiritually while serving as your pastor or minister? Why or why not?

Denominational Leaders

1. Does your denomination track or monitor the health of its pastors, formally or informally? If so, what methods of monitoring do you use? As leaders, how do you know whether or not your local pastors are currently in good spiritual, emotional, or physical health?

2. If you answered no to question 1 above, do you understand your policy to be primarily reactive, instead of proactive? How might you move toward a more proactive approach to pastoral health and well-being?

3. How often does a wounded pastor move to a new location and then suddenly begin serving in healthy ways? Isn't it more likely that a wounded pastor will bring along an expectation of being endangered or attacked in the new setting? Despite the reality of the situation in the new context, that very expectation may become a self-fulfilling prophecy. Have you seen things develop in this way?

4. Does your denomination or organization have a "recovery" program for healing and restoring burnt-out pastors? What systems or programs do you have in place for targeting persons who are exhausted, worn out, depleted, and uncertain of their current calling, with the goal of providing structured, positive, spiritual counsel and help?

NINE

LEARNING
FROM
CLERGY
ATTRITION
PATTERNS AND PRINCIPLES

Walk a few kilometers with an ex-pastor, and you can't help but learn a few things along the route. You may be surprised to discover a heart for ministry that still keeps its cherished circadian rhythms, attuned to the dates of each Sunday on a given year's calendar. In the chrono-biology of pastoral service, such cycles run deep. Many ex-pastors report that on Sunday morning they miss the ministry most—climbing a few steps to the pulpit, opening God's Word, and teaching.

Some of these same men and women may tell you that they don't miss the preparation for those teaching times. One ex-pastor, now managing an insurance office, reports that he preaches three or four sermons a year now, and it seems just about right in his carefully considered opinion. He is one of a few lay leaders who substitute for their local church pastor during times of vacation or illness. He is on call for last-minute needs, but usually has months to prepare each message.

"I can preach a pretty good sermon if I only have to write three or four of them a year," the former minister smiles. "It's harder to do that when it seems like every other day is a Sunday. And as soon as you finish a good sermon, the clock is ticking until the next one. Tick-tock. Sundays come around so fast you can't really keep up with it. I did my best to prepare excellent sermons each week, but honestly, some weeks I preached leftovers. Some Sunday mornings I climbed into the pulpit with my inspiration tank reading "empty," and of course I had to preach anyway.

"Ironically," continues the same veteran, "sometimes I got the best feedback after preaching the messages that had involved the least preparation. I never did make the connection there, or figure out why a haphazard and last-minute message would resonate better than something that I had time to study, prepare, and polish."

What other ex-ministers miss most is the shepherding of the flock—the visiting, the caring, the incarnational virtue of being a calm and consoling presence in the aftermath of life's inevitable storms. Not a few of such ex-pastors gravitate into service in the hospital chaplaincy, holding on to a shepherding role while letting go of the more preparation-intense duties such as researching and writing a new sermon each week.

"I get to preach brief devotionals now," one former pastor tells us. "I speak at a nursing home nearby, once a month. Our small group at church has adopted that particular nursing home because it's close to our church campus. Four of us men rotate in sharing the speaking duties, with each one of us doing a devotional one Sunday afternoon during any given month.

"Instead of having only a week to prepare a thoughtful forty-five-minute message, I now have a whole month to distill an inspiring five- or ten-minute devotional. So I have much *more* time to prepare and reflect, and then much *less* time that I have to fill up with speaking and teaching. For me, at least, the difference is liberating.

"There is so much less pressure," he says with evident approval. "I can take my time, pick and choose, dig down and discover the best stories and the clearest examples for the points I hope to make. I can tailor my remarks to a specific group—older people who live in a nursing home—rather than having such a broad range of ages and backgrounds to try to connect with."

Yet another ex-pastor, who claims to miss those pesky weekly deadlines and the constant ongoing need to prepare teaching materials, tells us that he is busy writing a book. In his case a bright and scholarly mind will have a lot to contribute to the literature of pastoral ministry. We look forward to reading what he produces.

Walk a few kilometers with an ex-pastor, and you can't help but learn a few things along the route. Walk with a few dozen ex-pastors, one at a time, and you can't help noticing that there are similar patterns displayed in their diverse stories.

We began interviewing ex-pastors more than a decade ago, while working on a graduate degree program. For us, it was a season of learning and growing, as we sat down with godly, mature men and women who had left the pastorate for one reason or another. We listened and learned. We counseled and wept. We bonded with faithful servants who had taken "early retirement" on a non-voluntary basis.

Despite the inherent tribulation and sorrow that was revealed in so many of these stories, we valued the chance to learn—and in some cases the chance to be therapeutic listeners, honing our counseling instincts while praying for wisdom.

We went out for quite a few walks with ex-pastors during that season of study and research. Despite the resulting calluses and the tired feet, we were blessed by what we learned. Within this chapter, we'll sketch a contour map of this particular terrain, highlighting patterns and principles that can be springboards to further study.

Patterns in Clergy Attrition

The decision to exit from pastoral ministry is a complex one, and it is usually not reached without considerable soul-searching and introspection. After all, a pastor or minister often feels called by God into service, so the major question looming overhead is simply this one: Has God changed his mind?

It's a question that pastors are inclined to take seriously. When they are up against a difficult situation, or thinking about a choice to leave the ministry, they feel obligated to address the proverbial nine-hundred-pound gorilla in the room: How does God feel about this? What is God's will in all of this? What would God have me do?

Typically, the adults in the affected household—a pastor and spouse—will bear the brunt of this angst-ridden reflection. They will be praying together and talking together and earnestly seeking God's light. In some cases they may choose to be somewhat transparent with their children, especially if they have adolescents or teens at home. The prayer and conversation may become a family affair.

One way or another, the process takes time.

When a decision to leave the ministry is finally made, the announcement is not usually the result of a solo process of decision-making; it tends to be more of a duet. And increasingly the children are given a voice before any decision is final, so instead of a duet or solo we are hearing the exit music from a small ensemble. Yet when listening from a distance, no matter how many instruments may be playing, one hears themes and motifs in the music that share inherent commonalities.

1. There is usually more than one issue involved

In just a moment we will look at the one single issue that looms largest in a decision to exit from pastoral ministry. But before we do, it's essential to notice that a choice to quit pastoring is usually the result of multiple challenges and more than one issue.

"As the last straw breaks the camel's back," wrote Charles Dickens, echoing an Arab proverb from earlier times. The idea is clear and simple: A beast of burden can carry a very heavy load, but sooner or later one small addition will tip the balance. The beast will stagger, the load will fall, and the animal's back will be broken. This will happen not because of the weight of the straw but because of the combined weight of the burden as a whole. The beast is already labored and struggling, but eventually there is a breaking point—a point of no return.

There is the care for the flock, whether in sickness or in health. Among congregations with older members, there may be a steady stream of funerals to conduct, as the saints go marching home.

There is the constant drumbeat of responding to complaints or criticisms from those who are upset. At any given time someone is upset, and the pastor will hear about it. There is rarely if ever a season when an entire congregation is healthy, positive, and pleased with how the church is being run. Meanwhile, critics emerge who tend to be vocal and outgoing.

There is the need to manage and lead the elder board, or to cope with an elder board that is managing or leading badly. There is the need to recruit yet another slate of volunteers for the nursery or the Sunday school classes or the care of the physical plant.

There is the financial pressure faced by a congregation that may be dwindling down in size and numbers, and the separate but related financial pressure faced by a pastor and family who may be barely surviving on a small ministerial stipend.

There may well be internal burdens from within the pastor's own marriage and family circle. At times, due to the nature of the ministry, pastors may try to carry these burdens alone, rather than revealing their frailty to the very flock they are trying to serve and lead.

All in all, pastors bear many burdens, even on their best days in ministry.

After a while, the combination of these burdens may accumulate until the load can no longer be borne. There may be a specific tipping point, or a proverbial last straw, but the resulting decision to leave the ministry is usually the result of multiple issues and causes—not a single one.

2. Conflict in the church is a major factor in ministry exodus

The issue of conflict in the church trumps all other factors when considering clergy attrition. Most often this conflict is unresolved and ongoing; the pastor departs from a situation while it is still troubled. In such cases a succeeding pastor may quickly be embroiled in the thick of the battle, or perhaps a denominational supervisor will enter the scene to attempt resolution and healing.

Some pastors we interviewed left the ministry after—not during—an occasion of conflict. By the time they departed from the setting, the specific issues had been addressed and the conflict was no longer active and ongoing. However, these pastors reported feeling "depleted" or "used up" by the battles; these ministers decided that they did not have the energy to continue any longer, even though things had apparently settled down.

One of the more interesting sub-patterns in dealing with the theme of church conflict is this one: When pastors left the ministry after a difficult season of church conflict, very few had exit interviews during which they were given a chance to reflect on their own situation. In the midst of the intense heat of a major battle—and while still bearing the scars inflicted on these caring ministers as they attempt to resolve the conflicts—no one came forward to nurture and console the wounded healers. Interestingly, some of the wounded healers were offered other places to serve in a new setting. It is not clear what sort of thinking or strategy is visible here. Do we believe that the best healing for a wounded minister is a new assignment?

The ministers we interviewed were nearly universal in their insistence that training in peacemaking and conflict resolution was not among their ministerial tools. One of the lone exceptions to this trend told us, "I do pretty well in managing conflict unless I'm the one who is involved. When I'm directly involved in the conflict, it seems like all my training just flies right out the window. I get defensive, I get upset, and I tend to forget to use all the skill sets that I learned in my training."

In other words, even the few ministers who have been trained in the skills of conflict resolution may lose their effectiveness in the heat of battle, when they themselves are besieged and under attack. These few may know what to do, but the hostile environment they are facing can unsettle them at a core level, replacing their calm demeanor with anger, anxiety, passive-aggressive behaviors, or defensive reactions.

One former pastor remarked that he might have remained in ministerial service despite all the conflict, if he had been single. "I just refused to keep putting my wife through that, and my kids through that," this minister sighed. "If it had been only me that was affected, I might have kept going. I might at least have been open to a new pastorate somewhere else. But as it was, by the time we had served in two highly conflicted places, I wasn't ready to watch my wife and kids go through that all over again, in a new setting. It wasn't fair to ask them to do that again."

If we wanted to adopt one single strategy that would cause committed and caring pastors to exit the ministry and abandon their posts, the best strategy we could use might be to constantly stir up conflict in the church. By all appearances, the enemy of our souls is aware of this reality and is much at work to attack and discourage pastors in this way.

3. Margin is missing from the minister's financial life

Although only about half of the former pastors we interviewed identified financial issues as causative in their departure from ministry, almost all of them talked about financial stress in the context of making their decision. Even when finances were not identified as being a driver in the process, the lack of resources was a constant underlying contributor to a sense of unease and discontent.

One former pastor put it this way: "When I accepted my call, my wife and I had one child. We looked at the salary and the housing and the total package and we realized that we could just barely make it on what the church was offering us. Just barely.

"When our second child was born, there were a lot of expenses we couldn't cover in relation to that. My wife had a difficult labor and there were a lot of out-of-pocket charges that we had to carry. We didn't have the cash to meet the needs, so we ended up putting hospital bills and other medical charges on our credit card.

"Even though the crisis ended and our second child came home healthy, our credit card bill was sky-high by then. Plus we had another child in our home, which meant more formula and more diapers and more of almost everything else. We had barely enough money to pay the bills, and there was no way we could ever pay down the credit card debt.

"My third child was born healthy, while we were still serving that church. But when the third child came, my wife and I had a very long talk about our financial situation. We realized that if we kept serving the church, I would still be making about the same amount of money. We couldn't envision a future in which the church was going to come along and raise our salary by 20 percent, or 25 percent, which is about what it would have taken to help us get solvent again.

"We prayed a lot and we talked a lot. As a result of that, I reached out to some people, through my father-in-law, and I was offered a job working for a large company in another state. The pay and the benefits were more than double what I was making as a pastor—that part surprised me.

"We were praying about it but honestly, when I got the job offer and we looked at the numbers, I don't know how we could have turned that down. I don't know how anybody who was in our situation could have turned that down. I really don't.

"Was God disappointed in us? I guess part of me has always wondered that. But we ended up having a fourth child—our fourth and last—and with the new job we could manage our income and get by just fine. We have done well in life, financially, and now we're putting our kids through college and we can afford to do that.

"Quite frankly, if I was still a pastor, I don't see how any of my kids could get to college, and I don't know how we would have ever paid down the debt from just having our second child!"

Other pastors echoed similar themes. For a few of these, the lack of financial margin was a primary factor in their decision to leave the ministry and seek other means of employment. For most, constant financial pressure was just one burden among many.

To return to Dickens and the Arab proverb, while church conflict was usually the "straw that broke the camel's back," it is clear that financial pressures were part of the heavy burden that weighed down the camel's back until it sagged—and then finally broke.

4. Unrelenting criticism contributes to the departure

Garrison Keillor has made a nice living writing witty stories about life in the upper Midwest, where farmers and business people mostly keep their thoughts to themselves—unless they're upset about something. The stoic and reserved citizens of the imaginary Lake Wobegon don't seem to have much to say, unless and until there's a problem. Then somehow, some way, criticism gets voiced. Keillor is spot-on. It's funny as he writes it, though a bit less so if you are a pastor serving a congregation in which positive feedback is rare and negative feedback is constant and ongoing. Without pointing to any specific geographic region or any one religious tradition, suffice it to say that sometimes our churches can be places where compliments are passed out very sparingly, while complaints are aired loudly and often.

Many former pastors mentioned this as a factor in their decisions to leave the ministry and find other venues of service or employment.

"I couldn't do anything right," one middle-aged minister sighed as he talked to us about his own decision-making process. "If I wanted the church to love missions, they thought prayer was more important. If I wanted us to study the Old Testament, they thought God was more visible in the New Testament. It hardly mattered what I was doing or what my opinions were: It seemed like no matter what I proposed, it wasn't what they wanted to do."

This particular minister was following a popular preacher who had gone on to serve a larger, more visible congregation. Unfortunately for his successor, this previous pastor had visible, often-used musical talents that were a frequent feature of his sermons and services.

"He would be preaching a message, and then he would suddenly just break out in song and lead the congregation in singing," the successor told us. "By all accounts he had a beautiful singing voice. He would get blessed, or get to a high point in his message—and one minute he'd be talking, the next minute he'd be singing. Apparently, that was a very popular aspect of his ministry there.

"That's not me at all. To get to the point—I can't carry a tune in a bucket," the successor exclaimed with visible exasperation. "And the whole time I served there, I felt like I was constantly being compared to [my predecessor] who had that beautiful voice and that great gift for music.

"I can tell you—nobody broke out into song while I was preaching, least of all me! I think I preached pretty good sermons. But I didn't have that beautiful tenor voice to just start a chorus or begin to croon an old hymn of the church at an emotional moment or whatever.

"How could I compete with that? I was constantly being compared to him, and I was constantly coming up short in those comparisons. It felt like everybody in the congregation was looking at me—and remembering what they were used to—and in that mix, I was being judged as inferior or less than what they had before."

Not everyone follows a much-loved hero, but many pastors relate stories of getting a steady stream of complaints or criticisms, while receiving compliments only rarely—and then often generically.

"If I don't count the mumbling at the back door, such as 'Nice sermon today, Pastor,'" one former minister told us. "Then I can probably count the compliments I received on the fingers of one hand. I was there almost four years and I didn't get praise or thanks or compliments. I would get those generic back-door greetings, usually without eye contact, and maybe people were being sincere but I heard 'nice sermon' about like 'how's the weather?' or some other generic conversation piece.

"I didn't have people talking to me positively about specific points in my messages or specific ways I had blessed them or anything like that," this same pastor relates. "When we left the church—and left ministry—there were a few people who said some nice things about me and about my service there. But they didn't say those things until I was halfway out the door. I was glad to hear it, but it was too late to help."

An oft-quoted church proverb claims that in any congregation, 5 or 10 percent of the people will be upset at any given time. A related proverb asserts that if people aren't complaining, then you (as pastor) aren't doing your job. These maxims may be rooted in underlying truths, yet they are little consolation to a caring, compassionate minister who is doing his or her best, yet hearing little or no positive feedback.

A steady stream of negative feedback and unhelpful criticism tends to wear down the morale and confidence of even the most committed ministers. Over time, the "boo chorus" may seem to resonate more loudly than the faint echoes of random, occasional praise. The result is that pastors are vulnerable to feeling let down, disappointed, depressed, or ineffective in ministry. Over time, these feelings may contribute to a desire to leave the ministry altogether and find another line of work.

Principles for Clergy Retention

As we survey the landscape of clergy attrition, there are some common themes that merit our attention and study. If we care at all about ministerial retention, and if we believe that our human resources are among our greatest resources for ministry, then we need to do a better job of protecting those who serve. A few principles toward that end are as follows:

1. Pastors may need more training in conflict resolution

Across the board, former ministers told us that they lacked training in effective conflict resolution. Some of them believed that perhaps such training might have kept them in pastoral service, saving their ministry.

One former minister put it this way: "At my seminary, there was a huge focus on [a specific doctrine] that permeated everything we learned. That was a great advantage to us, I believe, because that doctrine is a core belief of our church.

"When it was time for us to graduate, we had oral comprehensive exams with three professors testing us. And honestly, much of the testing and many of the questions revolved around that same doctrine.

"Did we understand the doctrine correctly?

"Could we explain the doctrine clearly?

"Were we planning to live out the doctrine in our daily lives?

"To graduate from that seminary with a master's degree, I needed to navigate my way through that doctrine, and then I was tested a lot on that doctrine to make sure I would be faithful to it later."

He pauses for a moment.

"Please don't get me wrong here," he continues. "I think that specific doctrine is essential to our faith. I'm on board with it! But I graduated from that school having no idea at all how to deal with angry people or how to lead an effective church board meeting or what to do when there was open conflict that was dividing my congregation.

"I sat in a little room for my oral comprehensive examinations, and no one ever asked me if I knew how to defuse tension or help people communicate more effectively or make peace in a difficult moment.

"And if they had asked me, I would have had to tell them that there were no classes at the school that had prepared me for those kinds of issues and problems.

"When I got out into the pastoral ministry I could teach that doctrine very well. I could preach that doctrine very clearly. But I didn't know how to lead a board meeting well, and I had no idea how to handle it when the bullets were spraying around and when the burning arrows were flying across the room, aimed directly at my head."

If we care about preserving our human resources and retaining our pastors for ministerial service, it is clear that we need to pay more attention to this issue.

How can we better protect those who serve?

Correspondingly, our church elder boards and our denominational supervisors would also benefit from training in communication theory, conflict resolution, and group dynamics.

2. Ministerial compensation needs our full attention

While writing this book, we interacted with a district superintendent who is currently serving a large territory. We raised some detailed financial questions, looking for general answers—not specific information about any one setting or church.

"More than half of my pastors are currently bivocational," this active-duty superintendent told us. "And that is the clear trend of ministry on our district. If I continue in this role for another five or ten years, I think we'll be down to only a handful of churches that can pay their pastor a decent salary. The rest of the churches will either have a bivocational minister or no minister at all."

The superintendent was *describing* reality, not *prescribing* what he believed the church should do about ministerial salaries.

Is there a biblical prescription that is available to us?

First Timothy 5:17 reads, "The elders who direct the affairs of the church well are worthy of double honor, especially those whose work is preaching and teaching."

A variety of Bible scholars and commentators have voiced observations that the true meaning of Paul's recommendation ("double honor") is "double pay."

Setting aside the practical realities for a moment, if we doubled the pay of our ministers, would they be compensated at a level that would allow them to continue to serve?

Most churches seem fearful of overcompensation where pay is concerned. They make their errors on the side of holding back, rather than on the side of giving generously.

One young former pastor speaks candidly about this, with traces of irony clearly revealed in his conversation.

"I had a lot of business professionals on my board," this former pastor relates. "They would come to board meetings and they would be talking about their new tablets or their new big-screen TVs or their new SUVs or something like that. It was clear that they made very good money.

"We would get to a discussion of pastoral pay—once per year, as our denomination requires—and these same guys would be fretting about whether to bump my pay by $100 a month.

"I would sit there, praying silently, asking God to help me not be jealous of these guys and their jobs and their salaries," this younger former pastor continues. "I tried my best! But I couldn't get past the huge contrast between the 'lifestyles of the rich and famous' on my church board and the lifestyle they were imposing on me by keeping my pay low and relatively unchanged."

This minister's story is personal and anecdotal, and thus perhaps is not a system-wide indictment of pastoral salary reviews. Yet as you listen to the plea of this (now former) minister, do you hear anything that sounds familiar from your own experience with church boards?

If we believe that our congregations are best served by having pastors that are bivocational, then we are already on the right course. We are heading in those directions and making steady progress.

If we believe that our congregations would be better served by ministers who were earning reasonable and realistic salaries—perhaps parity with local schoolteachers—then how might we move forward in the direction of healthier paychecks for pastors?

3. Pastors need positive reinforcement

Confession time: Both authors of the book you are reading were raised in Christian homes, by lay Christians who were active in, and highly supportive of, their local churches. Both authors of this book were raised by godly adults who supported their pastors and who said so out loud—often and repeatedly.

Pastors came and went. Pastors varied in styles of leadership and in gifts for ministry. Yet both of us, growing up in separate yet similar homes, witnessed godly men and women (our parents) who believed that it was their mission to support their pastor(s) through not only the good times but also the bad times.

How we need more such laymen in today's church!

Given the technologies in current use—text messages sent from cell phones, e-mail messages sent from tablets, and so forth—today's church-goers have a variety of ways they can express their gratitude and support directly to their ministers. Yet even in this battery-operated generation, a handwritten note of thanks still carries a lot of weight, and thus has a disproportionate value to the one who receives it.

One pastor of our acquaintance carries positive feedback (letters of appreciation, a variety of personal thank-you notes) in his well-worn Bible cover. He tells us, "When I'm feeling low, or when there's a voice on my shoulder telling me that my life doesn't matter or my ministry doesn't matter, I pull those notes out of my Bible cover and start reading feedback from people who have thanked me or written wonderful letters to me about my life or my ministry."

Can you put a value on that kind of expression? It's priceless.

Focus on the Family has led many congregations to observe October each year as Pastoral Appreciation Month. This is a wonderful and fragrant idea; it no doubt leads to gifts and celebrations that otherwise would not occur. Yet if we are serious about caring for those who serve us, perhaps we could appreciate them for twelve months out of the year, not just during October.

Ministers are always hearing complaints and criticisms. Maybe it's time for the "amen chorus" to raise its voice against the "boo chorus" and stand up for pastors with vocal, tangible appreciation and respect.

4. Ministerial retention should be a denominational priority

With seventeen hundred pastors leaving the ministry each month, there is clearly much more we can do in terms of ministerial retention. If we were making a serious effort to not only conduct healthy and positive "exit interviews" but also to actively counsel and consult with those who might leave the ministry, could we persuade a few hundred of these seventeen hundred to stay the course, remain in ministry, and keep serving?

Sometimes it seems as if we have better programs in place for "fallen" ministers—those who have made an ethical transgression or have been caught in a visible sin—than we have in place for pastors who quit because they are tired, discouraged, and weary of battle.

From time to time along our journey we have witnessed the case of a "wolf in shepherd's clothing" who goes through an established protocol for rehabilitation and a return to pastoral service. If we can do this for those who spectacularly "flame out" in ministry, why can't we find a better way to help those who merely "burn out" in ministry? Why do we have programs for one type of ministerial exodus (visible sin or ethical lapse) while we lack programs for good men and women who fall victim to snipers and critics and conflict? Where are the programs and protocols by which these good servants can find restoration, healing, and a pathway back into pastoral vocations?

Setting aside our love and respect for our ministers, we can frame this issue in sheer economic terms: It is far cheaper to retain an existing, already-trained minister than it is to train a new pastor from scratch. Beyond these economic realities, there is also a shortage of new recruits in the pipeline. Given a time of shortage, shouldn't we make even higher and better efforts to retain those who serve, thus retaining their value to the kingdom and to local congregations?

Studies confirm that frequent pastoral turnover is a contributing factor to congregational stasis, decline, or instability. By contrast, pastoral longevity tends to yield stronger, healthier (and yes, often larger) churches and congregations. Clearly, pastoral longevity is in the best interest of the local church and also of groups of churches such as denominations and movements.

If we are not willing to devote our resources to the care and retention of those who serve in ministry, we will continue to bear the fruit of our choices via pastoral turnover, pastoral exodus, and thus unstable and/or declining congregations. And for those denominations whose corporate existence relies in part on tithes, offerings, or budgets from the local congregation, do we not have a vested interest in the ongoing health (including fiscal health) of the many churches in our network, district, movement, or global denomination?

Efforts at ministerial retention should begin at the nearest level of contact and supervision, such as districts. The superintendent or bishop—whose motives and intentions probably already align with the idea of pastoral retention—should be trained in building quality relationships with the men and women who serve as pastors within the district or territory.

"These days, all good leadership is relational," says one busy district superintendent over lunch. "The days of having some kind of 'positional authority' over people are long gone. Today, if you want to be a leader of the men and women who serve as pastors on your district, you have to build meaningful relationships with them.

"If you don't have a relationship in place, you probably don't have permission to lead."

This particular superintendent has a proactive practice of staying in frequent, meaningful conversation and communication with the pastors who serve within his jurisdiction. Not surprisingly, his rate of pastoral turnover is very low, and his rate of pastoral exodus is virtually nonexistent.

"Leadership is relational, not positional," he reiterates.

"People trust me because I have built a long-term relationship with them and I have proved to be worthy of their confidence. If I was simply their boss, or the person at the next level up the chain of command, the trust wouldn't be there. And my leadership would suffer as a result of that."

Efforts at ministerial retention should begin at the level closest to the local congregation, yet would also prove valuable at levels such as university and seminary study, continuing pastoral education, and regional and global denominational offices.

NOTES

Chapter 1

1. "Statistics in the Ministry," Pastoral Care, Inc., accessed June 30, 2014, http://www.pastoralcareinc.com/statistics/.

2. Ibid.

Chapter 2

1. H. B. London and Neil B. Wiseman, *Pastors at Greater Risk* (Ventura, CA: Regal Books, 2003), 34.

2. Thom Rainer, "The Dangerous Third Year of Pastoral Tenure," thomrainer.com (blog), June 18, 2014, http://thomrainer.com/2014/06/18/dangerous-third-year-pastoral-tenure/.

3. Joseph Umidi, *Confirming the Pastoral Call: A Guide to Matching Candidates and Congregations* (Grand Rapids: Kregel Publishing, 2000), 13.

4. Glenn E. Ludwig, *In It for the Long Haul: Building Effective Long-Term Pastorates* (Bethesda, MD: Alban Institute, 2002), 89.

5. Ibid., 47.

ABOUT
THE
AUTHORS

Dr. David and Lisa Frisbie jointly serve as the coordinators of Marriage and Family Ministries for the global Church of the Nazarene. They also serve as the founders and co-executive directors of The Center for Marriage & Family Studies in Del Mar, California. Although they engage across a broad spectrum of family topics, they have invested much academic attention and professional study regarding issues of clergy marriages, military marriages, and remarriages/blended families.

Dr. and Mrs. Frisbie are the authors or co-authors of twenty-five books about topics in marriage, parenting, relationships, and family life. Among their more recent titles published by Beacon Hill Press of Kansas City are *Dating after Divorce: Preparing for a New Relationship* (2012) and a two-book set for premarital counseling: *Right from the Start: A Premarital Guide for Couples* and *Right from the Start: A Pastor's Guide to Premarital Counseling*, both of which were released in 2011. These and other books among their many titles have been published in Spanish, Portuguese, Russian, and other languages.

David and Lisa have published dozens of articles in journals and are frequent contributors to *ParentLife* magazine, published by LifeWay. They are regular columnists for *Refreshed* magazine, published by the Christian

Examiner group. Their articles on family topics also appear *in Grace & Peace, Holiness Today, Rev, Outreach, BabyLife* and other print and online publications. Dr. and Mrs. Frisbie are frequently quoted by other authors on topics of single parenting, divorce recovery, and a complex assortment of issues involved in remarriage, blending a family, and growing a healthy stepfamily. Dr. and Mrs. Frisbie enjoy writing and speaking on these topics and do so constantly.

Widely recognized and often quoted about issues of marriage and family life, Dr. and Mrs. Frisbie have traveled extensively to teach, speak, and train counselors, ministers, and leaders, in all fifty states of the United States, nine of Canada's provinces, and more than forty world nations. They have an active interest in serving pastors, missionaries, and other leaders and have been featured presenters at retreats and conferences for pastors and missionaries in North America, Europe, and other settings globally. They have also served and helped with candidate screening, orientation, debriefing, and member care of field workers and leaders for various NGOs and para-church organizations. They also serve as resource persons—speakers, counselors, facilitators, and event planners—in presenting retreats for teen PKs, MKs, and TCKs in diverse settings and places.

In their work for the Nazarene denomination, Dr. and Mrs. Frisbie are under the leadership and guidance of Larry Morris, director of Adult Ministries for the global church. They serve under the auspices of Sunday School and Discipleship Ministries (SDMI), which is led by Dr. Woodie Stevens. They also serve the USA/Canada regional office, which is led by Dr. Bob Broadbooks. David and Lisa provide writing, editing, teleconferences, web copy, consulting, speaking, teaching, and training for a wide range of Nazarene settings and situations. They are sought out and consulted by district superintendents and leaders of various district ministries. They enjoy being speakers and presenters at events including General Assembly, PALCONs, TEACH conferences, District Sunday School and Discipleship Ministry Conventions, and District Ministers and Mates Retreats, among many other venues.

Dr. David Frisbie is an ordained Nazarene minister who has performed more than four hundred weddings to date, in venues within the United States and also in other nations. In this capacity, he has led premarriage counseling sessions for couples from many cultures and of many different nationalities. Both David and Lisa travel constantly; both are lifelong learners with a great appreciation for cross-cultural experiences. Whether hiking across the Great Wall of China or sipping an espresso in Sofia, Bulgaria, these two adapt, adjust to, and learn from their local contexts and settings. They often say that they are "global Christians" rather than "North American Christians"—a cultural difference that is important to them.

Dr. David Frisbie is an adjunct faculty member at Southern Nazarene University, where he teaches courses in marriage and family life for the graduate and professional studies program. In addition, Dr. Frisbie has taught and lectured at colleges, universities, and seminaries worldwide, including teaching classes in premarriage counseling and pastoral counseling. Dr. Frisbie also holds adjunct professor status at Point Loma Nazarene University and at Oklahoma Wesleyan University and has been a guest lecturer at MidAmerica Nazarene University.

Both David and Lisa are alumni of MidAmerica Nazarene University; David has served as an elected member of the Board of Trustees for MNU. In addition David is an alumnus of Nazarene Theological Seminary in Kansas City.

David and Lisa have been named and quoted in USA Today, the New York Times, the St. Paul Pioneer Press, and numerous other newspapers. They have been interviewed on ABC-TV and CBS-Radio nationally. They have been interviewed on local and national radio broadcasts including Chuck Bentley's "Money Life" program and the "Focus on the Family" radio broadcast.

Author appearances and book signing events are held at secular bookstores including independent retailers and major accounts such as Barnes & Noble, in addition to Christian stores such as Mardel, Parable, Lifeway, Berean, Family Christian Stores, and more. Beyond these venues they do author appearances at church bookstores and at conventions and meetings of global Christian publishing organizations. Both David and Lisa serve as book judges for the Evangelical Christian Publishers Association (ECPA). They have done speaking, personal appearances, and book signings at global events sponsored by the Christian Booksellers Association (CBA) as well as the ECPA and at the annual conference of ICRS—the International Christian Retail Show.

Married since 1978, David and Lisa travel constantly to speak, teach, and counsel. Their life focus is helping marriages and families become healthy; they have a special heart for serving the marriages and families of pastors, missionaries, and others in full-time Christian service. This current book is a labor of love for these two, and springs out of more than two decades of serving and helping those who serve in direct, front-line pastoral ministry as well as those who serve in other contexts, such as cross-cultural ministry and church planting. Interviews and surveys for the book were conducted across a wide range of settings.

Further information is available on the Church of the Nazarene global website under the caption of "The Discipleship Place." Among other resources available at this site, Dr. and Mrs. Frisbie have authored a thirty-one-day devotional for married couples that can be accessed at no charge by registering at the site. The topic of the devotional series is "31 Days to a Stronger Marriage," and the material includes scriptures, personal stories, and insights drawn from their counseling experiences.

More information about these authors is also available via the business network LinkedIn. To make contact with the Frisbies, or to learn more about their publications and speaking ministry, access their business and professional profile on the business network LinkedIn, which is located at http:www.LinkedIn.com/in/davidandlisafrisbie.

To reserve a speaking event with these authors, contact Lisa Douglas—mountainmediagroup@yahoo.com.

For publicity, media events, and book signings by these authors, contact Laurie Tomlinson—Laurie@keymgc.com.

Also by David and Lisa Frisbie:
Managing Stress in Ministry (Beacon Hill Press of Kansas City, 2014)

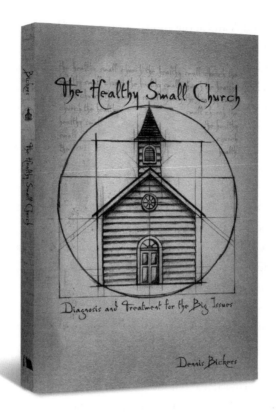

The Healthy Small Church diagnoses those things that can threaten the life of the church and prescribes practical remedies for treatment. In it, author Dennis Bickers helps your church become a healthy church that:

- Has a positive self-image
- Shares a common vision that creates purpose and unity
- Maintains community
- Practices the importance of faithful stewardship and financial support
- Encourages everyone to serve according to his or her spiritual gifts

---

The Healthy Small Church

ISBN 978-0-8341-2240-6

To order go to

www.BeaconHillBooks.com

BEACON HILL PRESS
OF KANSAS CITY

stress: (noun) a state of mental tension and worry caused by problems in your life, work, etc.

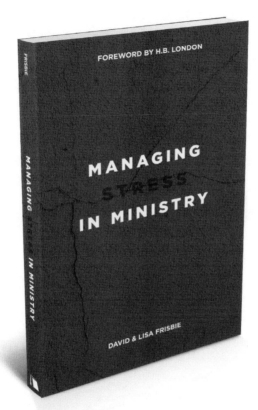

From role ambiguity and performance anxiety to financial scarcity and the complex realities of bivocational ministry, people in ministry face unique stresses. With real-life stories and concrete strategies, the Frisbies help pastors and their families identify and cope with the key stressors that impact the health of their ministries and their personal well-being. A much-needed resource for anyone in ministry.

Managing Stress in Ministry
David and Lisa Frisbie
ISBN 978-0-8341-3220-7

Available online at
BeaconHillBooks.com

BEACON HILL PRESS
OF KANSAS CITY